D1119965

THE WAY
PEOPLE
LIVE

Life in a Medieval Monastery

Titles in The Way People Live series include:

Cowboys in the Old West
Games of Ancient Rome
Life Among the Great Plains
  Indians
Life Among the Ibo Women of
  Nigeria
Life Among the Indian Fighters
Life Among the Pirates
Life Among the Samurai
Life Among the Vikings
Life During the Black Death
Life During the Crusades
Life During the French
  Revolution
Life During the Gold Rush
Life During the Great
  Depression
Life During the Middle Ages
Life During the Renaissance
Life During the Russian
  Revolution
Life During the Spanish
  Inquisition
Life in a Japanese American
  Internment Camp
Life in a Medieval Castle
Life in a Medieval Monastery
Life in a Nazi Concentration
  Camp
Life in Ancient Athens
Life in Ancient China
Life in Ancient Egypt
Life in Ancient Greece

Life in Ancient Rome
Life in a Wild West Show
Life in Charles Dickens's
  England
Life in the Amazon Rain Forest
Life in the American Colonies
Life in Communist Russia
Life in the Elizabethan Theater
Life in Genghis Khan's Mongolia
Life in the Hitler Youth
Life in Moscow
Life in the North During the
  Civil War
Life in the South During the
  Civil War
Life in Tokyo
Life in the Warsaw Ghetto
Life in War-Torn Bosnia
Life of a Medieval Knight
Life of a Nazi Soldier
Life of a Roman Slave
Life of a Roman Soldier
Life of a Slave on a Southern
  Plantation
Life on Alcatraz
Life on a Medieval Pilgrimage
Life on an African Slave Ship
Life on an Everest Expedition
Life on Ellis Island
Life on the American Frontier
Life on the Oregon Trail
Life on the Underground Railroad
Life Under the Jim Crow Laws

Life in a Medieval Monastery

by Victoria Sherrow

Lucent Books, P.O. Box 289011, San Diego, CA 92198-9011

Library of Congress Cataloging-in-Publication Data

Sherrow, Victoria
    Life in a medieval monastery / by Victoria Sherrow.
        p. cm. — (The way people live)
Includes bibliographical references and index.
    ISBN 1-56006-791-8 (alk. paper)
    1. Monastic and religious life—History—Middle Ages, 600–1500—Juvenile
literature. [1. Monastic and religious life—History—Middle Ages, 600–1500.
2. Monasteries.] I. Title. II. Series.
    BX2461.2 .S47 2001
    271'.009'02—dc21   00-010389

Contents

Discovering the Humanity in Us All

Books in The Way People Live series focus on groups of people in a wide variety of circumstances, settings, and time periods. Some books focus on different cultural groups, others, on people in a particular historical time period, while others cover people involved in a specific event. Each book emphasizes the daily routines, personal and historical struggles, and achievements of people from all walks of life.

To really understand any culture, it is necessary to strip the mind of the common notions we hold about groups of people. These stereotypes are the archenemies of learning. It does not even matter whether the stereotypes are positive or negative; they are confining and tight. Removing them is a challenge that's not easily met, as anyone who has ever tried it will admit. Ideas that do not fit into the templates we create are unwelcome visitors—ones we would prefer remain quietly in a corner or forgotten room.

The cowboy of the Old West is a good example of such confining roles. The cowboy was courageous, yet soft-spoken. His time (it is always a he, in our template) was spent alternatively saving a rancher's daughter from certain death on a runaway stagecoach, or shooting it out with rustlers. At times, of course, he was likely to get a little crazy in town after a trail drive, but for the most part, he was the epitome of inner strength. It is disconcerting to find out that the cowboy is human, even a bit childish. Can it really be true that cowboys would line up to help the cook on the trail drive grind coffee, just hoping he would give them a little stick of peppermint candy that came with the coffee shipment? The idea of tough cowboys vying with one another to help "Coosie" (as they called their cooks) for a bit of candy seems silly and out of place.

So is the vision of Eskimos playing video games and watching MTV, living in prefab housing in the Arctic. It just does not fit with what "Eskimo" means. We are far more comfortable with snow igloos and whale blubber, harpoons and kayaks.

Although the cultures dealt with in Lucent's The Way People Live series are often historically and socially well known, the emphasis is on the personal aspects of life. Groups of people, while unquestionably affected by their politics and their governmental structures, are more than those institutions. How do people in a particular time and place educate their children? What do they eat? And how do they build their houses? What kinds of work do they do? What kinds of games do they enjoy? The answers to these questions bring these cultures to life. People's lives are revealed in the particulars and only by knowing the particulars can we understand these cultures' will to survive and their moments of weakness and greatness.

This is not to say that understanding politics does not help to understand a culture. There is no question that the Warsaw ghetto, for example, was a culture that was brought about by the politics and social ideas of Adolf

Hitler and the Third Reich. But the Jews who were crowded together in the ghetto cannot be understood by the Reich's politics. Their life was a day-to-day battle for existence, and the creativity and methods they used to prolong their lives is a vital story of human perseverance that would be denied by focusing only on the institutions of Hitler's Germany. Knowing that children as young as five or six outwitted Nazi guards on a daily basis, that Jewish policemen helped the Germans control the ghetto, that children attended secret schools in the ghetto and even earned diplomas—these are the things that reveal the fabric of life, that can inspire, intrigue, and amaze.

Books in The Way People Live series allow both the casual reader and the student to see humans as victims, heroes, and onlookers. And although humans act in ways that can fill us with feelings of sorrow and revulsion, it is important to remember that "hero," "predator," and "victim" are dangerous terms. Heaping undue pity or praise on people reduces them to objects, and strips them of their humanity.

Seeing the Jews of Warsaw only as victims is to deny their humanity. Seeing them only as they appear in surviving photos, staring at the camera with infinite sadness, is limiting, both to them and to those who want to understand them. To an object of pity, the only appropriate response becomes "Those poor creatures!" and that reduces both the quality of their struggle and the depth of their despair. No one is served by such two-dimensional views of people and their cultures.

With this in mind, The Way People Live series strives to flesh out the traditional, two-dimensional views of people in various cultures and historical circumstances. Using a wide variety of primary quotations—the words not only of the politicians and government leaders, but of the real people whose lives are being examined—each book in the series attempts to show an honest and complete picture of a culture removed from our own by time or space.

By examining cultures in this way, the reader will notice not only the glaring differences from his or her own culture, but also will be struck by the similarities. For indeed, people share common needs—warmth, good company, stability, and affirmation from others. Ultimately, seeing how people really live, or have lived, can only enrich our understanding of ourselves.

"Life Orientated Toward God"

The Middle Ages (500–1400), especially the years between 500 and 1000 (known as the Dark Ages), was a stormy period in European history. Peace and order were in short supply after the fall of the Roman Empire in 486, as tribes of invaders from the east and north laid waste to one region after another. These tribes, including the Vandals, Visigoths, and Huns, were collectively known as barbarians and were feared for their cruelty and destructiveness.

Medieval people spent their time securing the basic necessities of life.

Plagues and famine also occurred regularly during the medieval era. Natural conditions—seasons, climate, the hours of daylight and night, distance, and terrain—controlled people's lives much more than they do today. A strict class system determined how most people would live and die, depending on their inherited place in the social order.

Medieval people worked hard just to survive, and most spent their time securing the basic necessities of life. Ninety percent of all Europeans in the Middle Ages were peasants who worked land that was owned by others. Members of the nobility, backed by personal militias composed of knights, kept busy protecting their lands as well as administering their estates. This meant that few people had time to pursue intellectual and cultural activities such as literature, the arts, or science, much less leisure activities. Fewer still were inclined to help the less fortunate.

A Powerful Influence

Under these conditions, civilization can stagnate and decay. However, another powerful force was at work. The Christian religion had been spreading, particularly after 380, when Theodosius made it the official religion of the Roman Empire. The Catholic Church became increasingly well organized and politically influential.

Christian doctrine appealed to many medieval Europeans and offered some stability

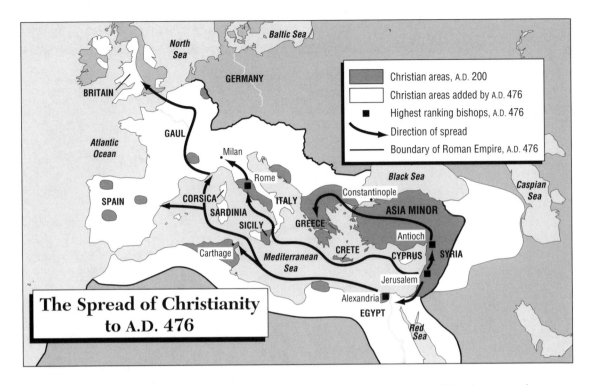

The Spread of Christianity to A.D. 476

Legend:
- Christian areas, A.D. 200
- Christian areas added by A.D. 476
- Highest ranking bishops, A.D. 476
- Direction of spread
- Boundary of Roman Empire, A.D. 476

in a disordered and dangerous world. Christians, who accepted Jesus Christ as God's son and their savior, spoke of peace, justice, and brotherhood, and said that all people were equal in the eyes of God. Their assertion that anyone who lived a good life and followed God's laws, through the agency of the church, could have happiness in the life to come after death offered many people hope and comfort.

In addition, the Catholic Church assumed many of the secular functions that the Roman imperial government had previously carried out. These included education, the judicial system, and help for the sick and poor. The church dominated life during the Middle Ages, giving the majority of Europeans a common frame of reference.

Retreating from Society

Long before the Middle Ages, some people felt a strong need to escape from the materialism, immorality, and lawlessness they saw around them. They craved a quiet and intensely spiritual way of life, free from the distractions of society. Those who chose to live alone and spend their time praying or meditating were called hermits.

The urge to withdraw from society was not a new phenomenon. Since ancient times, some men and women had deliberately isolated themselves in order to serve a higher power. They engaged in prayer and meditation and frequently fasted. Individual Jews are among the first known hermits, and practitioners of this solitary form of piety can be found today in Asia, Africa, and the Americas as well as in Europe.

Well before the time of Jesus, people who were drawn to the hermit's life began banding together in isolated places. These small groups, whose members offered one another protection from roving bandits as well as spiritual support, were the first monastic communities.

One well-known Desert Father— "Anthony the Hermit," later St. Anthony (251?–350?) —is sometimes called the founder of Christian monasticism. The son of a wealthy family, Anthony was inspired to give up his possessions, including a tract of fertile land, and live as an ascetic. Although he spent most of his life in his desert retreats, he did go to Alexandria to help Christians who were being persecuted there. At times, Anthony lived in a tomb, at other times in the ruins of a small fort or a palm tree located near a spring. He ate fruits he found in the wild, along with vegetables that he grew, and a bit of oil and olives that people brought him. The hermits who followed Anthony in the desert lived in separate cells and only joined together on Saturdays and Sundays for religious services. Many of Anthony's followers lived in group homes, called monasteries, and wore plain sacklike garments belted around the waist.

St. Anthony, sometimes called the founder of Christian monasticism, lived a life of prayer and simplicity.

Christian monasticism began in Upper Egypt, during the third century A.D., according to historical records. Following the example of Jesus (who often left his disciples behind so that he could pray in solitude), some men withdrew from the world and pursued a life of prayer and asceticism—that is, utter simplicity. They lived alone as hermits, also called anchorites. Because so many religious recluses went to the deserts (in the Middle East and Asia Minor), they came to be known as the "Desert Fathers."

The Desert Fathers' emphasis on solitude, or eremitism, became one of the foundations of monastic life. The other key element was in contrast, communal life—cenobitism. As different monastic orders developed, they worked out their own ways of balancing solitude with communal life.

Organized Communities

During the second and third centuries, more men joined the hermits and small groups formed communities based on lives of prayer and manual labor. People called them monks, from the Latin word *monachus*, which comes from the Greek word *monos*, meaning "alone." A few of the monks were ordained priests, authorized to administer the sacraments of the church and carry out clerical duties assigned by church officials.

By the fourth century, some monks were pursuing their spiritual goals in an organized and disciplined way, living together in walled enclosures called monasteries. During this time, under the leadership of men the church later declared to be saints, monasteries were built in various parts of Europe and Asia. One of the most influential of these men was Basilius, or Basil (ca. 330–379), who founded several monasteries in Greece. Basil urged monks to live in communities rather than as hermits. He said, "The solitary life has one aim, the service of the needs of the individual."[1] His monks ate together, prayed together seven times a day, and followed a schedule of work. The so-called Rule of St. Basil also called for charitable work, including the operation of orphanages.

The early monastic communities were self-sufficient, hiring no servants. Thus to make a monastery run smoothly, each monk was assigned a useful role and specific tasks. As a rule, monks lived simply on a diet of bread and fruit during the week with the addition of cooked vegetables on Sundays, but rules and lifestyles varied from one monastery to another. During the fifth century, John Cassian, who founded monasteries in present-day France, said, "We see almost as many types and rules set up for use as we see monasteries and cells."[2]

A Vital Role in History

During the Middle Ages, many new towns developed around monasteries, just as they had around castles and fortresses. People felt safer living near these walled compounds, and they knew they could receive certain kinds of assistance at a monastery. Under these conditions of well-earned public support, monasticism continued to expand and the movement became much more organized, ultimately playing a key role in medieval social development and progress. The prominent historian Arnold Toynbee has called monasticism "the matrix of Western civilization."[3]

Monks were well positioned to make significant contributions to society during the era. They reduced their own needs to the minimum and cultivated personal discipline. Their lives followed a predictable daily routine, within monastery walls. This allowed them time for prayer and other devotional activities as well as intellectual pursuits. Many monks spent hours every day reading, writing, teaching, and studying Latin, Greek, and other languages. Before the invention of the printing press, monks called scribes handcopied books and manuscripts for other people to read. They preserved the knowledge of ancient times and the writings of the Arabs, Greeks, and Romans, thus paving the way for the Renaissance. Many monasteries became centers of learning and the arts.

Monastery estates were well cultivated and productive, even those that were situated on poor-quality land. Monks developed

By devoting many hours to study, contemplation, and teaching, monks contributed greatly to society.

resourceful ways of irrigating land and clearing swamps. As both workers of the land and well-educated and thoughtful people, many monks both developed improvements in tools and work methods and described their gardening and farming techniques in writing. Society in general benefited from this innovation and instructions.

Monks also served as spiritual examples. Their focus in life was meant to be primarily spiritual, not material. The ideal monk was charitable, obedient, humble, and pious. Monks fulfilled certain social needs, praying

for people's well-being, caring for the sick and dying, housing travelers, teaching, and helping the poor. People living around monasteries who saw this exemplary way of life regarded them as religious role models and inspirations.

Benedicta Ward, editor of a collection of sayings of the Desert Fathers, sums up the monk's outlook: "To be in a true relationship with God, standing before him in every situation—that was the angelic life, the spiritual life, the monastic life, and the aim and the way of the monk. It was a life orientated toward God."[4]

Schools for the Lord

At 2 A.M., bells pierced the silence of the monastery at Monte Cassino in Italy. Monks rose from their hard mattresses, donned their shoes, and left their dormitory (sleeping area) for the chapel. There, they chanted psalms and heard readings from Scripture. This was the service called Matins, the first of eight periods of communal worship that marked their daily routine. For the rest of the day, the monks would read or copy religious texts or carry out other work-related chores inside and outside the monastery. The service known as Compline would finish the day. Then the monks would sleep until they were called to rise once again for Matins.

These men had joined together in a common search for God, and they lived in what their founder, now known as St. Benedict of Nursia, called "a school for the Lord's service."[5] Through prayer, the study of religious works, manual labor, and obedience to their abbot, or leader, and the monastic rules, they hoped to reach spiritual heights.

The monastery at Monte Cassino, a large stone complex set on a mountain, was located on a site where the Romans had once built a religious shrine to honor their gods. Mountains have traditionally been regarded as the dwelling place of supernatural beings. In this isolated place, Benedict intended that Monte Cassino would become a community unto itself. Founded in the Early Middle Ages, this monastery would serve as a model for thousands of others built in western Europe during the Middle Ages.

Benedict Founds His Order

Monasticism had been a recognized movement for nearly two centuries when Benedict was born in Nursia, Italy, around A.D. 480. When he was eighteen, his parents sent him to Rome to further his education, but Benedict was dismayed by what he considered the immoral behavior he witnessed there. He left Rome and secluded himself in the town of Subiaco, about forty miles away. There he encountered a monk named Romanus who spoke to him about religious matters and showed him to a cave. Benedict lived there for three years, spending his days in prayer and contemplation.

Benedict's pious ways attracted followers and he founded some small religious communities. Around the year 529 he led some of his followers to a mountain where he owned property. After obtaining permission from the local bishop, as required by church law, he founded the monastery at Monte Cassino, which was larger and more organized than the small houses he had established earlier.

The monks transformed the old Roman temples and other buildings into a church and living quarters, and built additional structures as needed with the stone that was plentiful in the region. A chapel was at the heart of Monte Cassino and its activities. On its south side was a cloister, a square area enclosed by sheltered walkways. Here, the monks gathered at certain times of the day to stroll, work, pray, and meditate, as well as meet at times when socializing was permitted. A small room with a hearth

Benedict (center) meets with members of his order.

The Rule of Benedict

Benedict thought carefully about the best way to organize and guide his community. He aimed to establish rules that were strict enough to provide order and discipline yet reasonable enough to encourage monks' adherence. He wanted not followers who were submissive or obedient because they feared punishment but rather spiritually vigorous men. To achieve these goals, Benedict tried hard to balance the practical with the idealistic.

Over time, he set down his vision of how the monks would live together and worship God. This set of principles and regulations became known as the Rule of Benedict (or, Rule for Monks). Benedict's Rule came to have such widespread influence that the great architect and medieval historian Viollet-le-Duc called it "the most important document of the Middle Ages."[6] Women who pursued the monastic life as nuns adapted the Rule to suit their own needs and communities.

Benedict's biographers Leonard von Matt and Dom Stephan Hilpisch claim that Benedict had special qualities that enabled him to develop a workable set of rules: "a healthy realism, an acute power of observation, a genius for organization, an unerring knowledge of human nature and a sound judgement." They conclude, "With all his idealism, Benedict never failed to make allowance for human weakness and the limits of individual capacity."[7]

The Rule of Benedict insisted that monks adhere to certain virtues, including obedience, humility, patience, and charity. They were to maintain silence most of the time as they carried out their activities so that they could stay focused on spiritual matters. Above all, they would sing the praises of God. They would meet in the chapel to chant psalms throughout the day and night and listen to religious readings, in addition to devoting themselves to private

located off the cloister provided one of the few places where the monks could warm themselves in cold weather. A garden was situated in the center of the cloister, a word that has come to symbolize monastery life.

Other buildings surrounding the cloister, which was situated so that it received the afternoon sun, included dormitories, where the monks slept, and small, sparsely furnished rooms called cells for private study and meditation. In addition to a kitchen and refectory (dining hall), Monte Cassino grew to include an infirmary, a scriptorium (writing studio), workshops, storehouses, and a brewery. Outside, the monks set aside land for a cemetery and planted gardens and cultivated fields.

prayer and study. The monks would also spend time at work each day and would, in Benedict's words, "ply their crafts with all humility."[8]

The Spread of Monasticism

Growing numbers of people were drawn to live as monks. Women were also drawn to the monastic life and women's orders developed along the same lines as those for men. They followed a similar schedule for worship and took similar vows. Groups of monastic women, known as nuns, lived in group homes, called convents, priories, abbeys, or monasteries. However, women's religious orders received much less financial assistance and fewer gifts than their male counterparts so they tended to be smaller and less prosperous. Some double monasteries (with separate living quarters for men and women) also existed.

Although many types of monasticism were practiced when Benedict founded Monte Cassino, his Rule gained support, especially among members of the church hierarchy. New Benedictine monasteries were established throughout Italy, and the movement spread to other parts of Europe, including the British Isles.

During the Early Middle Ages, Ireland became a major center of monasticism. Most Irish monks lived in looser associations than did monks in Italy; many groups chose deserted locations where they occupied individual stone cells grouped around a chapel. They spent little time together, gathering only for a daily service and a discussion of necessary tasks. Columba (521–597) strongly influenced Irish monasticism. Although he left no written rule, certain rules were attributed to him and his followers later wrote them down. They included these instructions:

The Ladder of Divine Ascent

A book called *The Ladder of Divine Ascent* (*The Ladder*) inspired many medieval monks. It lays out thirty steps (*logoi*) that call people to strive toward spiritual perfection. These steps (in memory of Jesus' life before his public ministry) guide readers on a path that is meant to help them aspire to "things on high." By submitting to God's grace, one can hope that virtues such as humility and charity will emerge and that his image will shine through. For example, Step 26 says: "Let us try to learn Divine truth more by toil and sweat than by mere word, for at the time of our departure [death] it is not words but deeds that will have to be shown."

The Ladder was written by a monk named John Climacus (also known as John Scholasticus) (A.D. 579–649?) of the Mount Sinai Monastery, which is located in present-day Israel at the site where, according to the Old Testament, Moses saw the Burning Bush and heard the word of God. John arrived at the monastery at age sixteen and took his vows about three years later. For about forty years, John lived as a hermit. He was well educated and spent many years studying the lives of the saints and writing about religious matters. Other monks regarded him as a holy man and sought his guidance.

Today, this work is read in Orthodox Christian monasteries each day of the Lenten season during the daily meal. It is regarded as one of the most influential works on spiritual life in Eastern Christendom.

Follow alms-giving before all things.
Take not of food till thou art hungry.
Speak not except on business.
The love of God with all thy heart and all
    thy strength.
The love of thy neighbor as thyself.[9]

Monasticism had a strong ally in Pope Gregory I, also known as Gregory the Great (ca. 540–604). Gregory, a Roman of noble birth, had once been a senator and military officer. Inspired by religious ideals, he sold his personal property and distributed it to the poor and entered a Benedictine monastery. Later, Gregory founded several monasteries and served as the abbot of one of them.

When he became pope in 590, the western church based in Rome was in a weakened state as a result of disasters that affected all of Europe, including invasions, floods, famine, and plagues. In addition, a divisive conflict with the eastern church was escalating. (The two branches would formally split in 1054.) Gregory believed that monasteries would serve to strengthen the church throughout Europe. He gave them tax exemptions and

"Life to Your Service": Bede the Venerable

An English monk known as Bede the Venerable (672?–735) is the first person to write scholarly works in the English language. He entered a Benedictine monastery at Wearmouth at age seven and later moved to the nearby monastery of Jarrow in Northumberland, where he spent nearly all of his life. He took his monastic vows at age nineteen, and became a priest at age thirty.

In addition to translating the Gospel of John into the English of his day, Bede wrote numerous hymns and letters and some forty books, mostly about theology and history, but also on subjects such as astrology. His most famous work is the *Ecclesiastical History of the English Nation*, which covers events from the Roman occupation of England through the year 731. Near the end of his life, Bede wrote these words, found in *The Catholic Encyclopedia*:

"I have spent the whole of my life within that monastery, devoting all my pains to the study of the Scriptures, and amid the observance of monastic discipline and the daily charge of singing in the Church; it has been ever my delight to learn or teach or write."

When he died at age sixty-two, Bede's possessions—a few handkerchiefs, some incense, and a few peppercorns—were given out to his fellow monks, as he had requested.

Bede the Venerable was a prolific writer who spent his entire life in a monastery.

Pope Gregory I sends missionary monks to England to spread Christianity and establish new monasteries.

put them under the direct control of the papacy, with certain autonomy, however; for example, other church officials, such as bishops, were not permitted to hold religious services inside the monasteries. Pope Gregory also said that laypersons—that is, a member of the laity, a believer who was not one of the clergy—could handle secular affairs for the monasteries so the monks could steer clear of such worldly matters. Furthermore, he encouraged wealthy people to support monasteries and worked to keep monasteries out of political controversies.

Missionary Monks

Pope Gregory and his successors also encouraged monks to convert members of the pagan tribes to Christianity and he sent them to various regions to make converts and to set up new monasteries. The missionary monks were inspired by the words of Jesus to his followers as found at the end of the Gospel of Matthew: "Go ye into all the world, and preach the gospel to every creature" (Matthew 28:19).

Throughout Europe, monks worked diligently to spread their religion, and, along with it, stability and literacy. Pope Gregory sent a pious Italian monk named Augustine to convert the Angles and their king, Ethelbert, to Christianity. In 596, Augustine led a group of forty monks across the English Channel from France into England. There, he met with Ethelbert. According to *Ecclesiastical History* (Book I:25), Augustine's representatives told the king that "he had come from Rome bearing the best of news, namely the sure and certain promise of eternal joys in heaven and an endless kingdom with the living and true God to those who received it."[10] The king permitted Augustine and his monks to preach to the people and to settle in Canterbury, where in 602 they built a monastery in the place where Canterbury Cathedral now stands. Augustine was its first archbishop.

During the sixth and seventh centuries, English monasteries were the homes of well-known abbots, scholars, and religious reformers. The monasteries at Wearmouth and Jarrow, in northern England, were particularly

King Ethelbert (seated, left) allowed Augustine (center) to settle in Canterbury.

distinguished. One famous monk who lived and worked at both of them was the scholar and medieval historian Bede the Venerable, who introduced the practice of dating events from the birth of Christ. The fifth-century apostle Patrick went to Ireland, where he and his followers, including Wilfrid, converted the Celts to Christianity. They also introduced books and a practical written language to Ireland. Many of Columba's followers were also ardent missionaries who converted people in Wales and Scotland and other parts of northern Europe, including parts of present-day France and Switzerland. Boniface went to Germany and established numerous monasteries in that country, which had been populated by non-Christians. Other well-known

missionary monks included Ansgar in Scandinavia, Adalbert in Bohemia, Swithbert and Willibrord in the Netherlands, and Emmeran in present-day Austria. In many cases, Christianity spread outward from the monasteries into the surrounding areas.

Continuing Growth

The popes who succeeded Pope Gregory the Great in the early seventh century continued to support monasteries and encourage their development. During those years, the leaders of the western branch of the Catholic Church declared as its standard the Benedictine monastery and Rule of Benedict. (The eastern branch, based in Constantinople, also had an important monastic tradition, which for centuries has influenced practices elsewhere.)

Important political leaders and monarchs also lent their support and sought to influence the development of monasteries in their kingdoms. One of them was Charlemagne (742–814), King of the Franks and later emperor of the Christian empire of the West, later the Holy Roman Empire. In the early ninth century, Charlemagne set out to regulate the monasteries under a central authority. One of the monks he most admired, Benedict of Aniane in southern France, later served as an advisor to his son, Louis the Pious. In 817, Benedict led a conference of abbots who met in Aachen, in present-day Germany, where Charlemagne had based his kingdom. These abbots formally accepted the Rule of Benedict, but initiated some changes. For example, they declared that agricultural work,

formerly mandatory, was henceforth optional, and that monks would be required to perform new duties of prayer and worship each day.

Monasteries continued to sprout up all over western Europe, usually in small towns or open country, sometimes in coastal areas. Missionary monks continued to play a significant role in converting people to Christianity. By the eleventh century, monasteries could be found in Spain, Portugal, Poland, Bohemia (present-day Czech Republic), Austria-Hungary, Sweden, Norway, Germany, France, Switzerland, England, and Ireland, as well as in Palestine and Greece. Monasteries were often named for their founders, their locations, a famous resident monk, or a particular saint.

During the twelfth century, Otto, bishop of Bamberg (Germany), established so many monasteries that critics advised him not to spend any more money on these projects. But Otto justified his mission:

Charlemagne (seated, left) was an influential force in the development of monasteries in his kingdom.

This whole world is a place of exile; and, so long as we live in this life we are pilgrims to the Lord; wherefore we need spiritual stables and inns, and such resting-places as monasteries afford to pilgrims . . . and lastly, I do all this for the full honor of God and for the succour of my neighbours."[11]

Expanding Roles

As monasticism spread, monasteries became more varied in terms of their size and functions. They assumed new roles that reflected the conditions in the surrounding communities and the changing times. A number of monasteries had more contact with the outside world than Benedict had envisioned.

Some monasteries grew quite large and included hundreds of monks. Two hundred was not an uncommon number. Around A.D. 800, the monastery at Fulda, in present-day Germany, housed about four hundred monks. Very large monasteries were known as abbeys; smaller communities were called priories. Often, small monasteries were affiliated with a nearby abbey.

Monasteries also varied in terms of their rules and routines. Although Benedict had said that monks would engage in manual labor and not emphasize scholarly activities, that also

Many English monasteries were destroyed during the Viking raids that began during the late eighth century. Their remote locations made them vulnerable to such attacks, and by 880, most of these monasteries lay in ruins. The invaders forced the monks to seek more protected areas, farther inland. Some monks had to flee to a new location more than once, carrying with them the sacred objects from their monasteries.

changed as many monasteries evolved as centers of education and literary activities. Other monasteries became more involved in housing travelers or caring for the sick.

By the mid-to-late Middle Ages, many monasteries stopped adhering carefully to the rules their founders had laid down. Critics complained that many monks were too materialistic. Although individual monks could not own property, they could hold possessions in common, as an institution. Some monasteries became much wealthier than others. The monks in these communities lived in grander surroundings and could enjoy fine food and other amenities that were at odds with their vows of poverty.

By the tenth century, people in all walks of life had observed that many monks had abandoned their original goals. Critics called for a return to strict observance of Benedictine rule.

Reform Orders

Some reformers created new monastic orders. One of the most prominent reform orders was based at the Cluny monastery in eastern France. Its influence eventually spread throughout the region and into Italy and Spain. Cluny was founded in 910 on a fine piece of land, including hunting grounds, donated by Duke William of Aquitaine, who expected the Cluny monks to strictly follow Benedictine rules. The monastery was also meant to be free from the control of local kings or noblemen.

Bertho, the first abbot of Cluny, and his successor, Odo, laid the groundwork for a large association of monasteries. Odo sent monks to found new, smaller houses under Cluny's authority, so that it expanded into a large and powerful institution, with vast real

The Cluny monastery in France became one of the largest and most influential of the Benedictine monasteries.

estate holdings, many servants, a renowned library, and grand surroundings. Despite these amenities, Odo expected his monks to be chaste, eat a simple diet, follow a strict schedule for worship, and speak only at certain times of the day.

Until about 1109, the Cluny monks adhered to the rules under which they had been founded. At the same time, the abbots made the monastery a showplace; according to one observer, they "marvelously adorned the cloisters with columns and marble brought from the farthest parts of the province."[12] They believed that beautiful sculpture, painting, and architecture should be used to glorify God's house. This attitude could also be seen in the small monasteries that were affiliated with Cluny. By the twelfth century, the Cluny monks also had changed their daily routine and spent most of their time in worship. The choir at Cluny sang devotional music for hours at a time. Servants performed much of the manual labor.

Founded in 1084, the Carthusians, another reform order of monks, were especially strict. Before organizing the Carthusians, their founder, St. Bruno, left the large cathedral of Reims, in present-day France, to live as a hermit in a wilderness area outside of Grenoble. Other men joined him, eventually building a new monastery in the mountains, where they felt close to God. Other groups of hermits joined them in the monastery they called the Grande Chartreuse.

Individual Carthusians spent most of their time alone, each monk even growing his own food and preparing his own meals. Carthusian monasteries were usually designed so that each monk lived in a small cottage with three rooms. Members of the order came together only for religious services or on certain days when group meetings were held, and they held themselves quite separate from the outside world. Carthusians were careful to screen new recruits carefully; they intended that their order would remain so steadfast that it would never need to be reformed. Their motto *nunquam reformati, quai nunquam deformati* means "never reformed because never deformed."

Double Monasteries

Sometimes groups of nuns and monks lived in religious houses that were located side by side and governed by the same leader, usually the abbot but sometimes an abbess, or nun. These double monasteries enabled the monks and nuns to share a common church building and the same priests. However, they followed strict rules of conduct. The men and women lived, ate, and worked in separate facilities but held joint religious services.

Double monasteries originated in the East and they date back to the early days of monasticism. Several double monasteries were founded in Gaul during the sixth century and the idea spread to other European countries.

St. Hilda (614–680) founded one of the best-known double monasteries. Hilda, a Benedictine nun, presided as abbess over both the monks and nuns at Whitby in England. Hilda was a well-educated woman who promoted education at the monastery and also became known as a patroness of the arts. According to Bede the historian, Hilda also exerted significant influence on church politics and both church and secular leaders asked her for guidance.

Despite the strictness of this order, it spread to other regions, notably throughout England. However, the Carthusians were the least numerous of all the orders. Historian G. G. Coulton estimates that they were "scarcely more than one-hundredth of the general monastic population."[13] People who saw the piety of these monks respected them and sought their prayers.

Still another major reform order, the Cistercians, was born in 1098. St. Robert of Molesme established the abbey of Citeaux, in southern Champagne, France. Noting the wilderness of the region, one observer described Citeaux as "a new monastery in a vast solitude, chiefly inhabited by wild beasts."[14] Robert named his reform group of monks Cistercians after the city of Citeaux and set out to return to the Rule of Benedict. People began to refer to Cistercians as the "White Monks" because they wore white habits, as opposed to the "Black Monks" (the Benedictines).

Cistercians rejected the idea of elaborate forms of worship or personal comforts and focused on individual prayer and study rather than group rituals. In addition, they regarded each Cistercian monastery as a separate entity, though all were united as one monastic order. They held an annual meeting so that the abbots from all the Cistercian houses could maintain their contact and uniformity. The abbot of Citeaux was permitted to visit any Cistercian monastery at any time to ensure that it was being run properly.

The Cistercians chose to locate their monasteries in austere and rugged surroundings. Under the Charter of Charity, written in 1118–1119, the Cistercians declared that their buildings would be simple, with no pinnacles, turrets, stained glass windows, or carved doors. Crucifixes were to be made of wood, not gold or silver, and the interiors should not contain carvings or wall hangings.

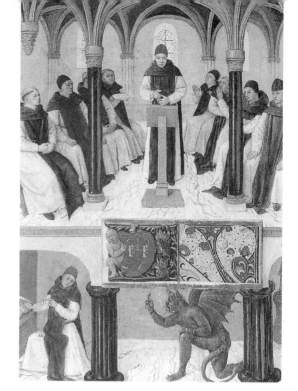

St. Bernard preaches to the monks of Clairvaux monastery (top). Satan tempts St. Bernard (bottom).

The early Cistercian monasteries were built like old Roman homes with four buildings enclosing a central square.

One of the best-known Cistercian leaders was Bernard, who founded a monastery at Clairvaux. Bernard was known for his long and frequent fasts and other forms of self-sacrifice. He was so charismatic and attracted so many new followers that, according to contemporary accounts, when he was nearby "mothers hid their sons from him, wives their husbands, and companions their friends."[15]

The various monastic orders continued to attract new members, and monasteries of various kinds appeared in new places throughout the Middle Ages. It is estimated that by the year 1415 there were more than fifteen thousand Benedictine monasteries alone. Throughout Europe, men willingly left behind worldly lives for the cloister.

CHAPTER 2

"Not an Easy Entrance": Joining the Monastery

Different monastic orders had different criteria for acceptance into the order, although they shared some of the same standards. The Benedictine order welcomed people from many walks of life, not just the elite. Benedict preached that different kinds of people all had something to offer; they could be peasants as well as educated nobles, rich or poor, young or old, priests or laypersons, so long as they had a strong desire to live in a religious community and obey the rules. In the Early Middle Ages, few monks were also priests. However, in 1311, church officials declared at the Council of Vienne that monks would be expected to proceed to take priestly orders, if their abbots told them to do so, "for the increase of divine worship."[16]

Men of different ages became monks. Some were young men who wanted to avoid the temptations and loose morals of the outside world. Some were older men who wanted to spend the rest of their days in prayer and good works. Others came because they wanted to live in a peaceful, structured environment or because they sought a secure home and companions. For a number of young men, monastic life offered the chance for an education and status they could never achieve otherwise.

While many men came voluntarily, some boys were given to the church by their parents. The monks themselves might suggest that a child be brought to the monastery if they noticed signs of great intelligence, piety, or other special qualities. Men who came to

A Knight Becomes a Monk

An account written by a medieval historian at Novalese (a French monastery) describes how an elderly former knight searched for the right place to take his vows. The knight had fought in many wars and "remembering the burden of his sins, thought within himself how to come to right penance . . . [by finding and] joining the monastery wherein the monks kept their Rule most strictly." In his book *Life in the Middle Ages*, G. G. Coulton recounts his journey:

"To whatsoever monastery he came, he would enter at the hour when the monks themselves came into the church to praise their God . . . then he would smite his staff twice or thrice upon the church pavement, that he might mark the strictness of their discipline by the sound of the bells that hung thereon."

At Novalese, he saw that the monks showed the piety he was seeking because they arrived promptly for services when the bells rang out. He stayed there and took his vows and later became the gardener at the monastery.

A mother offers her young son to the monastery.

the monastery at an early age often could not recall any other way of life.

Child Monks: Oblates

Young boys who were brought to the monastery by adults were called oblates. Generally, oblates were supposed to be at least seven years old, but a number of younger children were accepted. The vows of the child were considered binding.

Most oblates were the sons of freemen (people who were not bound to serve medieval landowners); others came from peasant families. Aside from religious reasons, some peasants simply could not afford to raise another child, or might want their son to have the opportunity to live a different kind of life and receive an education. When a serf (peasant bound to serve a landowner) gave his child to the monastery, the landowner was entitled to receive a payment from the family since he had lost a future worker. Emperor Charlemagne also set a limit on how many serfs from each region could enter the monastery: "The abbeys shall not receive too large a number of serfs, so that the villages may not be depopulated."[17]

Wealthy families had their own reasons for promising their sons to a monastery. Devout Christian families believed it was a blessing to serve the church. More pragmatically, a landed family might also send its second son to the monastery to prevent him from trying to displace the first-born son, who, under medieval laws, stood to inherit his father's property and title.

Initiation Rites

Oblates were received into the monastic order during solemn ceremonies inside the chapel. An excerpt from the procedure followed at the Abbey of Bec, in France, shows the initiation process:

> When any boy is offered for the Holy Order, let his parents bring him to the altar after the Gospel at Mass; and, after the Cantor [monk who led the chanting of the psalms] hath offered as usual, let the boy also make his offering. After which let the Sacristan [monk who was responsible for the acquisition and maintenance of monastic property] take the offering, and let the parents, drawing near, wrap the

boy's right hand in the altar-cloth. Then . . . let them give it into the hands of the priest, who shall receive the boy. . . . If they wish to make him a monk on that same day, let the Abbot bless his crown . . . pour holy water on his head, and, making the sign of the cross over it, crop his hair with the shears round his neck.[18]

At that point in the service, the boy would change into a monk's clothing. According to this text, when the boy reached the "age of reason" (usually around seven years) he would then make his vows with the other monks.

Oblates lived and dressed like the monks they would become.

Around the twelfth century, more people questioned the practice of expecting young boys to commit themselves to the monastery for life. They decided that when oblates reached the age of fifteen, they should be allowed to decide whether or not to remain in the monastery and take their final vows.

In many ways, oblates lived like the full-fledged monks they were expected to one day become. They wore smaller-size versions of a monk's clothing. They did not have individual cells but slept inside a group dormitory with other oblates. Oblates were required to attend the religious services and follow most other rules.

A Difficult Road

The road to becoming a monk was difficult, and adult newcomers were carefully screened. The obstacles were meant to discourage people who might not be truly fit for, or committed to, monastic life. Benedict instructed his monks not to admit newcomers quickly. Often, they had to knock repeatedly, waiting outside the monastery door for days without food or shelter from the elements. The monks who answered the door challenged a newcomer's sincerity and required the prospective monk to convince them of his faith. According to the Rule of St. Benedict:

> In the case of any one newly come to essay conversion of life, let not an easy entrance be accorded him; but as says the Apostle [Paul]: "Prove the spirits, whether they are from God." Therefore if any one who comes shall have persevered in knocking for admission and after four or five days shall have been found patiently to bear all the injuries inflicted upon him and the difficulty of gaining entrance and shall be

"What Manner of Tree?"

Young oblates often had more trouble than older novices or monks obeying the monastery's rules. Abbots complained about the difficulties of disciplining unruly boys who lived in the monastery. Some abbots authorized physical punishment as a means to convince oblates to follow monastic rules, but other abbots disagreed with these methods. In *Life in the Middle Ages*, historian G. G. Coulton reports that one frustrated abbot asked Abbot Anselm of the Bec monastery, "What, pray, can we do with them? They are perverse and incorrigible; day and night we cease not to chastise them, yet they grow daily worse and worse." Anselm advised his fellow abbots to refrain from beating young men: "Ye cease not to beat them? And when they are grown to manhood, of what sort are they then?" The other monk replied, "They are dull and brutish." Anselm suggested that

nurturing and loving guidance would produce better people:

"If thou shouldst plant a sapling in thy garden, and presently shut it in on all sides so that it could nowhere extend its branches; when thou hadst liberated it after many years, what manner of tree would come forth? And whose fault would it be but thine own, who hadst closed it in beyond all reason. . . . [P]erceiving in you no love for themselves, no pity, no kindness, no gentleness, they [the oblates] are unable henceforth to trust in your goodness, believing rather that all your works are done through hatred and envy against them. . . . The weakling soul, yet tender to the service of God, hath need of loving-kindness from others, of gentleness, mercy, cheerful address, charitable patience, and many such-like comforts."

---

found to persist with his petition, let entrance be granted him and let him be in the guests' house for a few days. After that, let him be in the novices' cell where he may meditate and eat and sleep.[19]

Acceptance as a novice was the first step in becoming a monk. Novices lived in the monastery for at least one year, sometimes more, before they were allowed to take their vows. A novice had to prove himself by following the rules of the monastery and keeping his first vows for the period of time set by his monastery. During that time, novices were in the care of a novice master, who watched and supervised them carefully. He taught them the rules and practices of the monastery and gave special encouragement to those who seemed especially promising. The novice

master and novices usually lived in the southern portion of the eastern cloister.

Benedict described the process by which a novice would be tested: "Let there be set before him all the hard and the rough things through which lies the way to God." After two months, the Rule would be read to the novice again, said Benedict, and these words should be spoken to him: "Behold the law under which thou dost wish to serve as a faithful soldier; if thou art able to keep it, enter; but if thou art not able, depart free."[20]

Knowing that some men might seek to enter the monastery to avoid military service, Emperor Charlemagne added this amendment to the laws governing monasteries:

Young men destined to monastic life must first pass their novitiate, and then remain a special religious ceremony, the monks made three solemn vows: poverty, chastity, and obedience. Benedict described the process in his Rule, saying that when a candidate was deemed suitable for the monastic life, for obedience and service to God, he could take his vows before the altar in the presence of the abbot and other monks. He would then sign his name on a written document that confirmed he had taken these vows.

During the ceremony, the monk received a special haircut, called the tonsure, and monastic clothing as symbols of his new status and responsibilities. The outfit, called a monastic habit, included a belted, cowled tunic and a scapular, a poncholike garment with three-quarter-length sleeves.

The monk made his vows not only to the order but also to the monastery in which he lived. This was known as the vow of stability. Benedict wanted the monasteries to be much like a family, whose members were connected to and committed to the community for life. To discourage men in his communities from leaving for other monasteries because they disliked certain people or conditions within their own house, Benedict wrote:

Once a novice took his final vows, he received a special haircut and a monastic habit.

in the monastery to learn the rules, before they are sent forth to fulfill their duties outside. Those who give up the world in order to avoid the king's service shall be compelled to serve God in good faith, or else to resume their former occupation.[21]

Professed as a Monk

A novice could become a monk by taking his final vows, which were binding until death. At

> Let him be received into the community, knowing himself to be now established by the law of the rule so that it is not lawful for him from that day onwards to go forth from the monastery, nor to shake free his neck from beneath the yoke of the rule which it was permitted him after such prolonged deliberation either to refuse or to accept.[22]

However, later in the Middle Ages, some monastic orders ceased to require their monks to stay in the same community throughout their lives. Individuals could ask for permission to move to other houses within their order.

A Demanding Life

Those who entered monastic life faced special challenges as well as opportunities. Monks gave up many personal freedoms, social connections, and ordinary pleasures. They had to leave behind their families and deny themselves the chance to marry and have children. Their days were highly structured, according to a schedule, and many rules governed their behavior. Usually, they could not choose the type of work they did but instead performed the chores that were needed in their monastic community as assigned. Their vow of poverty required them to give up personal property, according to the Rule of St. Benedict, Chapter XXXIII, which states:

A Distinctive Hairstyle

During the Middle Ages, the monk's hairstyle signified that he had entered a special world and devoted his life to serve the Lord. While most orders adopted some version of the tonsure, they did not all wear exactly the same style. In his book *Monks and Civilization*, historian Jean Decarreaux describes some of these variations. For example, he points out that Celtic monks, who recognized their monastic haircuts as a "mark of their servitude" to God, developed the following style, which differed from the Roman tonsure:

"Their heads were neither totally shaven, in the so-called manner of St. Paul, nor just the crown of them, attributed to St. Peter. They wore their hair long at the back and on the shaven frontal part of their heads a half-circle of hair from one ear to the other, leaving a band of hair across the forehead."

Although most monks wore the tonsure, the exact style varied according to the order.

Let not any one presume to give or accept anything without the abbot's orders, nor to have anything as his own, not anything whatsoever, neither book, nor writing-tablet, nor pen; no, nothing at all, since indeed it is not allowed them to keep either body or will in their own power, but to look to receive everything necessary from their monastic father. . . . Neither did any one of them say or presume that anything was his own.[23]

After taking their vows, monks were sometimes allowed to keep a few items on their person. These might include a rosary, handkerchief, sewing needle, razor for shaving their faces, and a personal bowl for eating, sometimes called a "begging bowl."

In return for these sacrifices, monasteries offered their members a safe and peaceful place to live, along with food and other basic necessities. Monks could develop their moral character and intellect, seek spiritual contentment, and find satisfaction in serving others. However, monks who failed to keep their vows and obey the rules were punished and sometimes banished from the monastery.

Obedience and Discipline

From the moment a monk entered the monastery, life was very different from life in the outside world. A monk gave up many personal freedoms and often had to suppress his own needs and desires to live in harmony with the group and the monastic rules. A monk's days were highly structured and focused on prayer and work. In most cases, he was expected to spend his entire life inside the monastery walls and to obey its leaders. Benedict regarded the virtue of obedience as closely related to humility; in his

Monks vowed to be chaste. Here, a monk burns his finger in order to resist temptation.

Rule, he wrote that "the first grade of humility is obedience without delay."[24]

A Cloistered Existence

The Rule of St. Benedict stated that monks should have little contact with the outside world. Benedict said that the monastery would contain and provide everything the monks needed "so that the brothers need never go outside, which can in no way be good for them."[25]

The monks also vowed to be chaste, and to help them avoid temptations in this respect, women were not allowed to enter the residential areas of men's monasteries. However, the monks worried that they might be visited at night by temptresses called succubi. One of the hymns they sang at the evening Compline service, before going to sleep, was a plea for protection from this sin:

> From all ill dreams defend our eyes,
> From nightly fears and fantasies;
> Tread under foot our ghostly foe,
> That no pollution we may know.[26]

Critics noted that certain monastic groups ignored one or more basic rules or applied weakened versions of them. By the Late Middle Ages, more monks were spending time away from the monastery. Some even became merchants and traders and others enjoyed traveling on a regular basis. Members of the

strictest orders criticized some monks for wan-
derlust that often took them away from the
monastery.

Dutiful monks spent their lives striving to
follow the rules inside their monasteries. To
promote peace and harmony and to keep the
monastery running smoothly, monks were expected to obey their leader, called an abbot,
whom they addressed as "father." The monks
called each other "brother" and were expected to treat everyone with respect.

A Worthy Leader

The abbot played a crucial role in the
monastery. Benedict declared that he was to
hold the place of Christ inside the monastery
and the monks must regard him as Christ's
representative in everything they did.

Returning to the Monastery

Occasionally, monks did have reason to
temporarily leave their monastery. Some
made regular trips to and from fairs or
markets to buy and sell items needed or
produced by the community. When a
monk returned from such a trip, the Rule
of St. Benedict specified the following
penitential procedure:

"When brethren return from a journey,
they should lie prostrate on the floor of
the oratory and ask for the prayers of all
for any faults that may have overtaken
them on their journey, such as the sight or
hearing of an evil thing or idol."

*The Benedictine abbot was the leader of the
monastery and considered to be Christ's
representative.*

Benedict and the founders of certain
other monastic orders declared that the abbot
should be elected by the other monks to serve
as their leader until the end of his life. In this
sense, monasteries were places in which every
member had some voice in administrative
matters. However, during the later Middle
Ages, popes, kings, and nobles often appointed their own abbots, many of whom
were not monks or even priests. In other

cases, people "bought" the position of abbot in order to gain power and control valuable monastic property.

A monk was bound to obey the abbot in all things, but the abbot, in turn, was expected to rule wisely and to consider the other monks' needs and opinions. He was supposed to treat people fairly and listen to the views of the other monks, which they could share during their group meetings.

Because abbots would wield so much power, Benedict carefully listed the qualities these leaders should possess. The Rule of Benedict says that an abbot should have a "worthy manner of life" and "fundamental wisdom."[27] He should, furthermore, teach by example and "show forth all good and holy things by deeds more than by words."[28]

Benedict further described the qualities he envisioned in an abbot:

It behoves (sic) him therefore to be learned in divine law, that he may thence bring forth things old and new; to be chaste, sober, merciful; and let him always exalt mercy above judgment, that himself may attain it. Let him hate the faults, let him love the brethren. . . . Let him not be too full of commotion nor anxious, jealous nor too suspicious, because such an [sic] one is never at rest. In the matter of the commands he gives let him be provident and considerate before God and man.[29]

Many abbots lived up to these high ideals and were widely admired for their principled behavior. Bede the Venerable described Easterwine, a pious abbot who served at the monastery at Jarrow during the seventh century:

Though he had been an attendant on King Egfrid, and had abandoned his temporal vocation and arms, devoting himself

A Visit from the Abbot

Abbot Odo ruled over the monasteries affiliated with Cluny in the tenth century. Not all the monasteries under his authority welcomed visits from this reformer. According to Marjorie Rowling, in her book *Life in Medieval Times*, one eyewitness later said that the monks at Fleury barricaded the entrance when they knew Odo was about to visit them. Monks stood on the roof of the building and appeared ready "to hurl stones and missiles at their enemy," while others guarded the door. This resistance lasted for three days. Odo then secretly returned to the abbey riding on a donkey and completely alone and unarmed. Impressed with Odo's humility and courage, the monks at Fleury then welcomed him.

to spiritual warfare, he remained so humble and like the other brethren, that he took pleasure in threshing and winnowing, milking the cows, and employed himself in the bakehouse, the garden, the kitchen, and in all the other labours of the monastery with readiness and submission. [As an abbot] he retained the same spirit, saying to all, according to the advice of a certain wise man, "They have made thee a ruler; be now exalted, but be amongsth them like one of them, gentle, affable and kind to all.". . . If he found the brethren working, he would join them. . . . He ate of the same food as the other brethren, and in the same apartment; he slept in the same common room as he did before he was abbot.[30]

In large monasteries, the abbots appointed other monks to help them perform

A Worthy Abbess

The female counterpart of the abbot was an abbess (the name given to the female superior for a community of twelve or more nuns). Her position was generally similar to that of the abbot but she had less authority to punish the nuns in her house and she was not permitted to preach or issue spiritual orders.

The nuns of the house elected their abbess, who was expected to be experienced and wise. According to the *Catholic Encyclopedia*, Pope Gregory the Great banned young women from being appointed as abbesses, and church officials at the Council of Trent later decreed that an abbess must have "completed the fortieth year of her age and the eighth year of her religious profession."

their duties. The abbot of a large Benedictine monastery of the twelfth century might have one or more assistants, called a prior, sub-prior, and third prior.

By the ninth century, critics noted that some abbots fell short of Benedict's ideal and did not follow the traditional guidelines. These abbots focused more on wielding power and using the monastery's material assets than on spiritual values. In some of the wealthier abbeys, abbots were installed with pomp and ceremony. They received a miter and ring and were greeted by knight vassals and the monks of the order, while festive music played in the background. Many abbots also enjoyed luxurious accommodations and more elaborate meals than their fellow monks and entertained guests in a grand style. Yet many other abbots worked hard to exemplify the virtues of poverty, chastity, and humility and to set a good example for their fellow monks.

Living by the Rules

Rules dictated even the most basic of a monk's daily activities, including when he was permitted to use toilet facilities. Monks were naturally expected to follow the Ten Commandments and the laws of the church. Proper behavior meant that a monk was not permitted to gossip about his fellow monks, show anger, quarrel, doze during a religious service, arrive late for worship services, or break the periods of silence. In addition, he was forbidden to speak to a woman except in special circumstances; for example, to conduct monastery business or care for the sick.

Silence was a form of discipline that the monks imposed upon themselves to encourage contemplation and inner dialogue. Monastic orders had different rules regarding silence, although they all prohibited casual or idle conversation. Some monks were required to be silent most of the time, while others might speak more often, even daily. Certain times during the day were set aside as silent periods.

Other rules detailed the occasions when speaking would be permitted; for example, when it was necessary to fulfill a work assignment or when the monks were dealing with guests. As such apparently minor attempts to circumvent the rules suggest, not all monks were completely obedient at all times.

Once again, Benedict emphasized humility in describing the ways that a virtuous monk would speak. He wrote, "The eleventh grade of humility is that a monk, when he speaks, speak slowly and without laughter, humbly with gravity, using few and reasonable words; and that he be not loud of voice."[31]

Talking was forbidden during meals. To communicate at these times, monks devised an extensive nonverbal "vocabulary" of signs that indicated what they wanted to communicate; for example, they made swimming motions

Monks who broke the rules were punished to encourage them to do better in the future.

with their hands to ask for a serving of fish. Historians have identified at least one hundred different signals the monks used at mealtime. In addition to hand signals, or in cases where using the hands was forbidden, the monks used their feet, and sometimes they whistled.

Even at times when the rules did not forbid speaking, monks were expected to refrain from making noises or disturbing the tranquil atmosphere of the monastery. They walked quietly, with bowed heads, from place to place.

Breaking the Rules

Monks who broke the rules had to acknowledge their mistakes and, in some cases, submit to punishment. In general, the Benedictine rules were designed to encourage monks who misbehaved to do better in the future rather than to give up in despair. Punishments were designed to suit the offense. For instance, a monk who arrived late for meals might have to give up his mug of wine and dine alone. Monks who failed to arrive on time for religious services were expected to experience the shame of being late.

Mount Grace Priory

Carthusian monasteries are known for their strict rules and emphasis on solitude. One surviving Carthusian monastery in England, Mount Grace Priory, has been preserved as a historic site and is located in a wooded area under the slopes of the Hambleton Hills.

When the monastery operated, each monk lived in almost total seclusion in a two-story cell that had its own running water and fire. The monks each had a small garden outside their cells and they prepared their own food. Inside these cells, they prayed and ate alone.

Monks who committed serious offenses were subjected to public punishment.

Penalties for talking out of turn were not usually extreme. The monk might be required to do extra penance, for example, although a novice might be struck across the face by the novice-master.

However, monks were supposed to take care to properly recite the psalms and other prayers during religious services. In his Rule, Benedict stated that anyone who made a mistake in these areas must "humble himself there before all, giving satisfaction [or] he shall be subjected to greater punishment, as one who was unwilling to correct by humility that in

which he had erred by neglect." Children who committed this offense "shall be whipped."[32]

A monk who committed a serious offense might have to endure public shame. At Cluny, for instance, a monk who told lies or falsely accused another monk of wrongdoing could be ordered to stand outside the chapel door in his bare feet without his hood on. A servant stood nearby to explain his misconduct to people who passed by. Monks who committed a misdeed might also be shunned for a period of time or be sentenced to lie face down on the ground while the other monks walked by.

The most extreme punishment was banishment from the monastery.

Group Business

The monks discussed matters of misconduct and punishment at group meetings, regular gatherings to discuss monastery business and make decisions. Regular meetings were scheduled each morning, according to the Rule of Benedict. This meeting was regarded as important for the spiritual well-being and smooth functioning of the group.

At Benedictine monasteries, the meeting began with readings from a chapter of the Rule of St. Benedict, in order, he wrote, that nobody "may excuse himself on the basis of ignorance."[33] A sermon was also read, for in those days of strict church authority with respect to doctrine, individual community leaders were not encouraged to write a new sermon every day. Rather, classic sermons by, for example, an order's founder, were read aloud, again and again.

Benedict never said that the monks needed a special place for their meetings.

However, a chapter house became part of most monasteries and the monks used it for their meetings. Chapter houses were so-called because meetings began with the reading of a "chapter."

During the meeting, monks received their orders and instructions for the day. Monks could also discuss problems affecting their group and express grievances against another. A monk could request forgiveness for any such wrongdoing. After the meeting ended, the monks might attend a private mass, do spiritual reading, or work until the next group devotional service, called Terce.

An abbot could call a special meeting when he wanted to consult with the entire group. Ultimate decision-making authority, however, rested with the abbot. Benedict wrote:

> As often as anything especial is to be done in the monastery, the abbot shall call together the whole congregation, and shall himself explain the question at issue. And, having heard the advice of the brethren, he shall think it over by himself, and shall do what he considers most advantageous."[34]

Daily Living

onastic life revolved around scheduled prayer, study, and work, activities performed in accordance with monastic vows. During a typical day, group and individual prayers and religious studies occupied about eight or nine hours and about six hours were allocated for physical labor, leaving nine or ten hours for eating and sleeping.

People inside the monastery carried out different roles and jobs, working together to fulfill the mission of the monastery and make it as self-sufficient as possible. In large monasteries, a great many people, not all of them monks, filled various roles to keep things running smoothly.

Managing Provisions

One or more monks were in charge of food and other provisions, which were stored in the granaries, barns, and cellars of a monastery. A monk called the cellarer handled these matters, as well as the buildings and rooms that were used for agricultural purposes. At times, he or his assistants went to fairs and markets to obtain food and other supplies, such as fuel. He also hired and supervised the servants who worked to prepare and cook food. The cellarer thus functioned as a sort of "head housekeeper" who made sure the monastery had adequate food and other domestic supplies to serve the monks, their servants, and guests.

In larger monasteries, the cellarer had one or more helpers. They included the subcellarer

and the granatorius (keeper of the grain), who was in charge of grinding and selecting grain for flour. Working with the cellarer, a kitchener determined how much food the monks would need for their meals. The kitchener was obliged to carefully document his expenditures and show these accounts to the abbot each

Cellarer monks shopped at fairs and markets for food and supplies.

In addition to the monks, lay brothers and servants worked in the monastery. For example, at the large Cluny monastery in France, the monks did not do much heavy manual labor, so laypeople did the outdoor work and other tasks, such as cooking. In the twelfth century, Peter the Venerable, abbot of Cluny, replaced the servants with lay brothers. The Cistercians in England also found lay brothers to help them work the land.

Lay brothers (called *conversi*) were adult males who came voluntarily to the monastery but did not become monks. Many of them had been farmers or tradesmen. The rules regarding lay brothers differed somewhat from one monastery to another. They did have to agree to follow certain rules of the monastery; for example, they took vows of obedience and gave up their material possessions. Even if they left the monastery, lay brothers could not legally marry. They could keep their beards and did not receive the tonsured hairstyle. Lay brothers also could not become members of the choir.

The monastery provided them with food and clothing. According to the *Cambridge Medieval History VII (1932)* (in Genevieve D'Haucourt's book, *Life in the Middle Ages*), the men who worked for the Abbey of Montebourg in Normandy in 1312 were each given: one loaf of bread, peas for soup, three eggs and $\frac{1}{4}$ a wheel of cheese or six eggs and no cheese, and as much wine from the monks "as they wanted or needed." During Lent, they were given three herring fish and some nuts.

week. Like the cellarer, a kitchener had to know how to read, write, and do arithmetic.

Benedict describes the person who would make a good cellarer as

> a man of mature character, self-controlled, not haughty, not easily moved to anger, not rough, not extravagant. Should a brother chance to make an unreasonable demand, he must not grieve him by a contemptuous denial but refuse the improper request on reasonable grounds. . . . Let him not fall into avarice nor waste the substance of the monastery—let him not keep the brethren waiting or treat them in a superior manner. Things must be done in such wise that "no one is troubled in the house of God."[35]

The refectorian handled matters relating to the dining room (refectory), keeping it clean and supplied with dishes, napkins, serving containers, utensils, and cloths. He also supplied towels and other necessities for the lavatories.

Monastery Meals

The monks grew their own food and helped prepare their own meals. In a traditional Benedictine monastery, each monk, from the abbott to the youngest oblate, took his turn in the kitchen. However, in some monasteries, lay brothers or servants prepared and served meals.

Professed monks ate in the refectory, while the oblates and novices ate together in a separate room. Dining tables in the refectory usually were arranged alongside three of the room's walls. Before entering the refectory, the monks washed their hands in a lavatory near the entrance.

Meals varied from one monastery to another. Here, Benedict and his monks dine on fish, bread, and wine.

In many monasteries, only one meal was served daily during the cold months. Young boys were given a midmorning snack of wine and bread. During the warmer months when the monks were working outdoors, they usually ate two meals to provide more energy for physical labor. However, some monasteries changed these rules and served more than one or two meals a day year-round.

Meals were austere in most monasteries. According to Benedictine rules, meat was forbidden; the monks were not to eat "meat of a four-footed beast"[36] except when they were ill. However, historians have observed that monks would sometimes pretend to be sick so they could enjoy meat.

Benedict had considered numerous details regarding the meals themselves. His Rule states that a monastery should serve more than one dish at every meal "so that he who perchance cannot eat of the one may make his meal of the other."[37] A typical dinner might consist of dried beans, prepared boiled and salted; cheese or eggs; and vegetables, usually from the monastery gardens. Carrots, onions, and leeks were staple crops in Europe during the Middle Ages. Bread and wine appeared at all meals. Some monasteries kept beehives for a supply of honey.

Fish might appear on the table on Thursdays and Saturdays, as well as on special religious fast days. Some monasteries raised carp in ponds located on their grounds, served as special dishes when dignitaries came to visit. Oysters, which were regarded as a humble food in those days, were usually served on feast days.

Changing Menus

During the later Middle Ages, meals were more varied from one monastery to another. Some monasteries permitted meat, as long as it was "hunted game," while others ignored the Benedictine rule forbidding meat. One critic charged that a certain monastery let dogs attack their pigs so that they could call the pork "hunted game." Records indicate that monks protested as a group when they disliked the kinds of meals that were served: to eat fowl, they cited the book of Genesis saying, "the waters bring forth abundantly, after their kind, and every winged fowl after his kind" (Genesis 1:20–21).

Poorer monks often subsisted on bread, water, salted fish, and the vegetables they raised themselves. In very lean times, they had only black bread and watered-down wine.

However, some wealthier monasteries served substantial dinners that included varieties of meat and fowl, as well as wines and cordials (including the special liqueur that is still made today at the Benedictine abbey in Normandy, in France). Sometimes higher-ranking monks were served more elaborate meals; a medieval history called the *Anseys de Mes*

Efficient Workers

Some monks devised ways to do their work that were more efficient than the standard medieval practices. Certain agricultural

methods, such as crop rotation, were developed or advanced by monks. They also found ways to use water power more efficiently for pumps, saws, and mills. Monks were especially adept at mobilizing water power. Cistercian monks often placed their monasteries over one or two streams. They used the flowing water to build a well that would provide cooking and drinking water and, at some distance, to carry away waste products. At Byland Abbey in England, Cistercian monks built the largest medieval earthen dam in the country. It formed a thirty-acre lake on land at the abbey.

During the twelfth century, monks at the North Yorkshire Abbey used water to power a type of blast furnace they designed and built to make cast iron. British archaeologists who examined the site of these ironworks during the twentieth century found that the monks had been able to make all-metal tools, instead of tools that were merely edged with iron or steel. These tools were important for the development of both agriculture and certain crafts.

Ruins of Byland Abbey in North Yorkshire, England.

includes a disapproving description of these developments:

> The monks drink in violence and strife of the best wines which God has established. They eat bread as white as hail; of all flesh do they eat also, so that their bellies are full and stuffed and they almost burst through the middle. But real [holy men] do not act so. They have bread of barley, kneaded with water, and wild fruit which they have gathered in the woods, and various herbs and roots, also.[38]

In 1179, the scholar Giraldus Cambrensis expressed his disdain after a visit to Canterbury, where he observed the lavish meals the monks ate. These included sixteen dishes with savory sauces and an array of beverages—ale, beer, mead, claret wine, and mulberry wine. But despite their sometimes lavish meals, the monks maintained a physical image of slightly shabby simplicity.

Grooming and Clothing

Medieval monks in Europe could be recognized by their hairstyles, clothing, and clean-shaven appearance. In the custom of the era, they seldom bathed; medieval Europeans lacked comfortable facilities for bathing and also feared that baths were unhealthy or could spread disease. The Rule of St. Benedict states that monks need not bathe often, unless they are sick. They did wash their hands and faces in the morning and washed their hands before eating, perhaps more out of respect for scriptural injunctions than from fear of contamination. They also usually washed themselves thoroughly once a week and took full baths before Christmas and

Typical attire for a monk included a habit, a cloak, and sometimes sandals.

Easter. Using simple razors, Western monks kept their faces clean-shaven.

The Rule also maintains that monks should wear "whatever is available in the area, or whatever is cheapest."[39] Thus they wore simple garments called habits, which resembled the outfits of poor peasants. They received new clothing as necessary. The Rule calls for the monks to have available these items of clothing: two cloaks (one for cold weather), two tunics (one for sleeping), a scapular or apron, belt, socks, shoes, and a handkerchief. In winter, monks in colder climates added sheepskin cloaks with hoods, along with boots and gloves with fur linings.

The basic ground-length tunic or robe was made of rough cloth, often wool or linen, either dyed or undyed, depending on the order. Novices usually wore undyed habits. This tunic, sometimes called a chemise, was belted with a simple cord. A drawstring pouch strung from this cord held the monk's rosary. The scapular was worn over the tunic, to which was attached a cowl, or hood, that could be pulled over the head. A rope was tied around this outer tunic. A simple pendant-style cross completed their attire. Abbots often added a ring and staff.

Some monks went barefoot as a form of self-sacrifice but many wore shoes or sandals, usually with socks, hose, or leg bindings. Stockings of some kind were necessary because monks of most orders were forbidden to show their bare legs. Some who worked outdoors did belt their habits above their knees for practical reasons, however. Monks who did outdoor work sometimes wore heavy shoes with thick soles.

The twelfth-century Cistercians were known for their extremely simple garments. A contemporary historian, William of Malmesbury, wrote that these monks did not wear breeches "unless when sent on a journey, which at their return they wash and give back. They have two tunics with cowls, but no additional garment in winter."[40]

One monk, called the chamberlain, made sure that his brothers had clean, serviceable clothing. Tailors working in the monastery shops made the items the monks needed and the fabrics for garments usually came from trade fairs. Worn clothing might be repaired or replaced; garments that the monks could no longer use were given to the poor.

"To Labor Is to Pray"

Because early hermits spent their time away from others and devoted themselves to solitary prayer and meditation, some religious men criticized their isolation as self-centered and uncharitable. The simple tasks, like weaving or light gardening, performed by early monks did not interfere with contemplative activities. Indeed, manual labor was an essential part of the early-fourth-century monasteries. According to Benedict, work of any kind was to be considered a prayer in honor of God. In his Rule, Benedict wrote, "Idleness is an enemy of the soul. To labor is to pray."[41]

Sometimes, the first physical labor monks had to perform was building their own monastery. Many monasteries began life as simple wooden shelters, which eventually were rebuilt with stone. When living quarters and a chapel had been constructed, the monks were assigned jobs as needed. Any kind of work—gardening, cooking, washing dishes, mopping floors, milking cows—was regarded as worthy, and a monk was expected to perform it with humility and good humor.

Historian Jean Decarreaux shows how the monasteries put their various resources to good use:

Monks built and managed their own monasteries.

The forests provided wood for building and heating, and, under the oak-trees pigs, for which there was an enormous demand outside the monasteries, fed on acorns. Goats and sheep provided meat and skins; where the land had been reclaimed cows and horses . . . cropped the lush meadows. Bees provided wax for church candles and honey for sweetmeats. There was no lack of cereals, which were cut by sickle and trampled down by horses at threshing-time. There were apple and pear orchards and kitchen-gardens for raising beans, lentils, peas and turnips. The vines produced communion wine, of which a great deal was drunk.[42]

Farming and Agriculture

Agriculture was the monastery's most common labor, necessary both to feed the members of the community and to provide other raw materials.

Preparing the land was often a big job, because as a rule, monasteries were located in wilderness, apart from society, or on land nobody else wanted because it was barren or swampy. Before they could till the soil to grow their food, the monks had to clear forests, drain swampland, or find ways to irrigate dry areas. The monks became so adept at cultivating land that some monasteries were famous for their excellent farms.

The Cistercians often built their monasteries in valleys, with good sources of water, and worked hard to turn swampy, marshy areas into good farmland. They were also known for their ingenious hydraulic systems. At their monastery Royaumont in France, a central channel moved water out of the latrines and also powered the waterwheel, as well as other machines used in the workshops. Cistercians at Maulbronn Monastery in Germany, founded in 1147, devised an in-

A Monastery Garden

One of the most famous monastery gardens can be found in the Swiss monastery of St. Gall, named for an Irish monk named Gallus who lived on the site as a hermit monk for thirty years during the seventh century. Gallus, known for his gardening skills, developed his version of the ideal Benedictine monastery, including four gardens, along with the plants that should be grown in each one.

The monks at St. Gall circulated his ideas during the ninth century. The four gardens, named for their unique purposes, were: cemetery, cloister, infirmary, and kitchen. Like the monasteries themselves, the gardens reflect two major goals: to serve God and humankind. The kitchen and infirmary gardens contained foods and herbs that would sustain and heal people's bodies. The cloister garden was a place of prayer and contemplation; cloister gardens were meant to be peaceful. Some of the more ornate gardens contained decorative fountains in the center. Flowers were also grown in the cemetery gardens where monks were buried. Often, plants on these grounds had special significance and were associated with "remembrance." Lilies and irises were among the flowers grown in these gardens.

Some large monastery gardens contained more than a dozen varieties of vegetables, along with vineyards and diverse fruits. The garden at Cluny contained grapes and other delights that appeared on the monastery tables.

---

tricate network of drains, irrigation canals, and reservoirs.

In addition, monks raised cattle, sheep, and chickens, and some became experts in animal husbandry. They also kept bees for honey and sometimes silkworms. Such high productivity often led to surpluses; for instance, one year an Italian monastery at Bobbio was able to sell "2,100 bushels of corn, 1,600 cartloads of hay, 2,700 litres of [cooking] oil, 5,000 pigs; large and small cattle . . . 800 amphoras of wine and other products."[43]

To supplement their cash crops, monks planted and maintained smaller gardens inside the monastery walls. These gardens contained ornamental plants or crops and herbs that were used in the kitchen and for making medicines. Flowers were cultivated to decorate the church and to lend beauty to the outdoor setting.

Although Benedict emphasized the importance of manual labor, fewer monks engaged

Since agriculture was their primary labor, many monks became proficient farmers.

in it during the Late Middle Ages. Monasteries with hefty endowments from neighboring nobles did not require monks to work in the fields or to perform kitchen chores and housework, and some monks came to regard such work as undignified. In the wealthiest houses, paid servants even took over the chores of shaving the monks' beards.

Adequate Rest

The excesses of the later Middle Ages notwithstanding, Benedict had expected the monks to be busy. Thus he provided in his Rule that they would receive enough sleep each night, around eight hours, although their sleep was interrupted by nighttime religious services. Sleeping schedules varied somewhat depending on the season of the year.

In the early monasteries, monks slept in a dormitory, and large monasteries held several sleeping areas. However, some monasteries changed their sleeping arrangements and provided individual cubicles for each monk. Each monk had a mattress (made from straw or rush), a sheet woven of rough cloth, a bed covering and pillow. They slept in their clothing so they would be prepared to rise and go quickly into the chapel for Matins. Cistercians went to sleep fully dressed, except for their cloaks.

Health Concerns

In other ways, Benedict showed concern for the health of the monks when he founded his order. He did not impose intense physical hardships on his monks or ask them to suffer privation in ways that could damage their health. According to medieval historian Norman F. Cantor:

The abbot was responsible for preserving the health of the brothers; he was to make sure that the monks had two solid meals a day and that the sick, young, and old received special care. . . . Benedict did not care much for the extreme forms of asceticism, such as flagellation, hair shirts, or prolonged fasting.[44]

Many monasteries followed the medical practice of bloodletting, which was believed to promote good health and relieve illness. For centuries, people believed that bleeding was an effective way to remove diseases from the body. The monks who cared for the sick performed this treatment on others and rou-

Benedict insisted that the monks in his order be well cared for, including receiving adequate sleep each night and medical attention if necessary.

Some monks found the rigid schedule and self-sacrificing life in a monastery unbearable and would leave, unable to fulfill their vows.

tinely received this treatment themselves. For example, at the Abbey of Saint-Germain des Pres in France, monks were bled five times a year. Most monasteries allowed monks to request a "bleeding license" issued by the abbot between four to ten times in a year. Bloodletting was banned around the times of major religious feast days and during fasts that could not be broken.

During a bloodletting, monks went to the infirmary or to a country retreat or rest home operated by their order. They bathed and rested during the day and slept more hours than usual each night. They were permitted to eat meat and socialize with each other. According to one report, during the bloodletting times, which lasted about three days, "the cloister monks are wont to reveal the secrets of their hearts."[45]

As human beings, monks were vulnerable to a range of physical and mental illnesses related to their vocation and lifestyle. Some became overweight as a result of eating a starchy diet paired with the lack of exercise that prevailed in some monasteries. Some monks became seriously depressed, a condition known in the Middle Ages as melancholia, or developed other mental illnesses connected with poor adjustment to life in cloistered surroundings, with its many restrictions. It was said that evil spirits could cause monks to experience these kinds of problems. One of these spirits was called the Midday Demon, who caused monks to question their way of life and tempted them to break their vows or return to worldly ways.

Monks who felt unbearably closed in or bored might seek out opportunities to leave for a monastic errand or pilgrimage. Some even left the monastery completely and became wandering beggars. They found cloistered life, with its rigid schedule of prayer and sacrifice, too demanding or confining to endure. Although they had taken binding vows, they could not fulfill these promises.

Daily Living **47**

"Watchinge unto God": Spiritual and Contemplative Activities

A monk's foremost duty was to pray in accordance with the sacred routine of his order as practiced in his particular monastery. Monks engaged in communal and private prayers (for their own spirituality and for the souls of humankind) and their personal reading of the Bible and other works of spiritual value. The well-known prohibitions on talking at certain times of the day were intended to encourage contemplation and inner dialogue.

Benedict said that the monastery was a house that should be always "watchinge unto God."[46] In his Rule, he set a schedule (Horarium) for his monks that included eight prayer services each day, called the Divine Office. Benedict referred to the Divine Office as Opus Dei, meaning "God's work," and he bid his followers, "Let nothing take precedence over the work of God."[47] Bernard of Clairvaux, the founder of a strict Cistercian chapter, told those who entered his monastery, "If you desire to live in this house, leave your body behind; only spirits can enter here."[48]

Special Roles

In addition to reciting their group and solitary prayers, certain monks performed special roles during religious rituals. Other monks took care of the chapel and the various items that were used for prayers and worship services.

Some important jobs in the monastery centered around its religious functions. The cantor, or precentor, directed the devotional services and the music, which was a vital part of Benedictine worship. One of his duties was to teach oblates and novices to chant properly. In addition, the cantor often served as the monastery's librarian and archivist. He took care of the choirbooks and, in some monasteries, the religious manuscripts. His other duties included selecting the religious material to be read at meals and notifying other monasteries of a death in his own monastery.

Some abbots also appointed an antiphoner to read at Matins each morning. The antiphoner read the first section of the psalms and certain other parts of the service. The "priest of the week," called a hebdomadarian, sang the high mass each day at monasteries where such masses were celebrated and gave the special blessings.

The sacrist tended the chapel itself, in particular its cloths and furnishings—altars, hangings, candles, lamps, bells, other physical features—and slept there at night to keep guard. He made sure the chapel was clean and properly adorned for religious holidays. Because the sacrist was in charge of lighting, he supervised the making of candles and obtained the necessary wax, tallow, and material for wicks. The sacrist also cared for the cemetery.

A sacrist sometimes had an assistant called a revestiarius, who took charge of the hangings

Singing was just one method of worship that monks engaged in to bring them closer to God.

and linens in the chapel and the vestments worn by the men who officiated during the services. The treasurer looked after church treasures such as the sacred vessels and reliquaries (containers of sacred relics, such as pieces of a saint's hair or bone). Together, these functions made possible the smooth performance of scheduled worship services each day.

Schedule of Worship

Each day, monks followed the Horarium, the schedule of short services at which they recited psalms, sang, and offered brief prayers. Communal prayers took up about four or five hours every day; an additional four or five

hours were set aside for individual prayer and religious readings, all designed to bring the monks closer to God. In the Early Middle Ages, mass was not said every day in the monastery, nor did the monks receive the sacrament of Holy Communion on weekdays.

Benedict ordered this schedule of eight daily devotional services at Monte Cassino; it was followed in most other monasteries. He gave precise details as to the order and composition of the psalms the monks would recite.

Services were held inside the oratory of the monastery chapel, which was usually built at the north of the complex. The sanctuary faced east, in the direction of Jerusalem, where Jesus had lived and died. The church bells would toll approximately every three

Monks worshiped together and individually for eight to ten hours each day.

hours around the clock to signal the beginning of another service.

Rising for Matins

At approximately 2 A.M. (sometimes earlier) came Matins. The monks rose from their beds to pray a series of psalms and read Scripture and other holy writings. In the later Middle Ages, Matins was held earlier or later to permit the monks a longer period of uninterrupted sleep. Benedict realized that his monks would need fortitude to rise so early each day to worship. In his Rule, he wrote, "When they rise for the work of God, let them gently encourage one another, on account of the excuses to which the sleepy are addicted."[49]

Monks required extraordinary powers of memorization, especially during the Early

Middle Ages when printing had not been invented and handwritten manuscripts were rare. Historian Morris Bishop offers a glimpse of their experience:

> Matins in the dark choir must have been very dramatic, with only a few wavering candles to illumine the lesson reader's book and reveal the high gloom of the choir, the outlines of cowled singers and carved saints. In the early days the monks had no lights for reading; they were required to know by heart both words and music of an enormous repertory of psalms, chants, anthems, and responses.

Changes occurred in the fourteenth century when candles became more available. Bishop continues:

> Thanks to the wider diffusion of wax candles and service books and the elabora-

tion of musical notation, reading replaced memorization. . . . Candles were fixed above the choir stalls, and a favorite prank of the monks was the dropping of hot wax onto the bald pate [head] of a drowsing comrade below.[50]

The Other Offices of the Horarium

Matins was one of eight services. Lauds, a hymn of praise, marked the dawn at about 5 A.M. Prime was a shorter devotional service and took place shortly after Lauds. The monks usually washed off in the lavatory before this service, which was followed by the daily group meeting.

Terce came at 9 A.M., after the meeting, while midday or noon brought Sixtus or Sext. Nones was held at about 3 P.M., and the monks gathered at 6 P.M. for Vespers, which means "evening" in Latin. Hymns, canticles, and psalms were part of this great Office, a service of praise and thanksgiving at the end of the day. Before retiring for the night, the monks met for Compline at about 9 P.M.

Benedictines traditionally followed this routine closely; other orders followed either the same routine or a modified version. Some monasteries held a service in the middle of the night, around midnight, at which a monk carrying a lantern walked around the chapel to make sure that all were attentive and no one was asleep.

Religious services could be quite long. For instance, the Matins or Lauds service at Canterbury Cathedral in the eleventh century was composed of fifty-five psalms. The monks were expected to stand while they sang the entire Office. More often, Matins consisted of one chant, three anthems, three psalms, and three lessons. It was during Matins, as well,

---

Raising the Soul to God

Peter Damian, an important eleventh-century reformer, who believed that some monks were not spending enough time on prayer and contemplation, suggested that his fellow monks regain a focus on the basic principles of monasticism.

"Therefore, dearest brothers, snatch up the weapons of sobriety, humility, patience, obedience, chastity, charity, and all the virtues, and do not concern yourselves over fields and cities, sons and wives, but only about your own souls, which rise above every other consideration. . . . You must above all fast and pray, since fasting will tame the desires of the flesh while prayer raises the soul to God."

"Preach with the Hand"

As scribes who copied books, monks performed a great service in medieval times. Cassiodorus, the former minister of Emperor Theodoric the Great and the founder of a monastery, encouraged this activity in monasteries. As quoted by historian Paul Lacroix in *Military and Religious Life in the Middle Ages and the Renaissance*, Cassiodorus praised their work with these words:

"Of all your physical labours, that of copying books has always been the avocation most to my taste; the more so, as by this exercise of the mind upon the Holy Scriptures, you convey to those who will read what you have written a kind of oral instruction. You preach with the hand, converting the fingers into organs of speech, announcing silently to men a theme of salvation; it is as it were fighting the evil one with pen and ink. For every word written by the antiquary, the demon receives a severe wound. At rest in his seat, as he copies his books, the recluse travels through many lands without quitting his room, and the work of his hand has its influence in places where he has never been."

that the monks would celebrate the feast of any saint whose day was about to begin.

Spiritual Nourishment

In addition to participating in the communal services, the monks were supposed to hear and read works of piety every day. These works were meant to provide spiritual inspiration to the monks and enhance their ability to chant the psalms. This aspect of monastic life required literacy, and many monks who could not read were taught by their fellows. At Monte Cassino, each monk received a book each year during Lent (the penitential season before Easter), which he was expected to finish reading by Easter.

In addition to the Bible, monks read stories of the lives of saints and books and papers

Often monks stood for hours, singing and chanting.

Monks were required to read every day in order to receive spiritual inspiration.

written by great monks. The works of Basil were available in Greek, those of other monks, such as John Cassian (or Cassianus), in Latin.

Historian Jean Decarreaux points out that in medieval times, people used both speech and hearing while reading. They read the words half-aloud and heard the sounds at the same time their eyes were taking in the text. Thus, says Decarreaux,

> meditation was not a matter of reflection, examination, or mental analysis, but the repetition of what had been read, spoken aloud and retained by ear. Such repetition, which was really a form of memorization, was a form of mental training and preparing the will to action.[51]

Devotional works were also read at meals. A monk called a lector read biblical passages, psalms, or accounts of the saints' lives. Works by famous monks, including John Cassian's *Collations*, were also chosen. Some refectories had a special built-in platform for the lector. The works selected always matched the season of the church year.

Special Religious Observations

For all medieval people, especially monks, the calendar was divided into the seasons of the church year. People did not speak of days in terms of months and numbers, but in relation to, for example, Advent (the period before

The Rule of St. Augustine, written in the fifth century, influenced the monastic orders that were founded in medieval times. This Augustine was the famous North African religious leader, who preceded Augustine of Canterbury by nearly two hundred years. As described in the *Catholic Encyclopedia*, he wrote specifically about prayer in Chapter II of his Rule:

"Be assiduous in prayer at the hours and times appointed.

In the Oratory no one should do anything other than that for which was intended and from which it also takes its name. Consequently, if there are some who might wish to pray there during their free time, even outside the hours appointed, they should not be hindered by those who think something else must be done there.

When you pray to God in Psalms and hymns, think over in your hearts the words that come from your lips.

Chant only what is prescribed for chant; moreover, let nothing be chanted unless it is so prescribed."

Christmas), Michaelmas (which marks the feast of one archangel Michael), or Lent (the penitential season before Easter).

Some holidays were especially important. A monk celebrated the feast day of his patron saint and Benedictine monasteries have traditionally said special prayers each year on the anniversary of St. Benedict's death. Lent, the weeks preceding Easter, was a period of fasting, penance, and serious meditation. Easter, which commemorates the resurrection of Jesus, was an occasion of great joy. Christmas, when Christians celebrate the birth of Jesus, was obviously another important holiday on the calendar. A contemporary account describes the way that holiday was celebrated at the Cluny monastery:

It was the custom of Cluny to celebrate the Saviour's Nativity with singular affection, and with more devotion than any other solemn feast; not only with melody of song, with longer lessons in church, with the light of multitudinous tapers [many candles], but (far beyond all this) with special devotion and copious shedding of tears, in joyful unison with the Angelic Host.[52]

Although monks engaged in a range of mundane activities when they were not praying or studying pious works, all actions were intended to bring them closer to God. Whether working in a garden, greeting pilgrims, copying a manuscript, or giving alms to the poor, the monk could offer these deeds as a work of devotion, performing them in the spirit of humility, obedience, and love.

Some monastic orders concentrated almost exclusively on spiritual activities, whereas others, especially later in the Middle Ages, focused more on charity, teaching, manual labor, or scholarly pursuits.

"Love Thy Neighbor": Good Works

When Benedict founded his monastery and developed his famous Rule, he envisioned the monastery as a community apart from mainstream society, a safe, and safely removed, haven for the pious. However, the Rule of St. Benedict did set forth these general principles in regard to serving others: "Let [the monk] take the greatest care of the sick, of children, of guests and of the poor."[53]

Over time, monks throughout Europe became more involved with the outside world and recognized the needs of the people who lived around them. Because monasteries were stable institutions with capable, industrious members, they had the resources to respond to certain problems. People also came to expect that monks, who had taken solemn vows to serve God, would follow the biblical instruction to "Love thy neighbor as thyself" (Matthew 22:39). They sought the monks' prayers and material help as well.

While some monasteries remained more aloof than others, many monasteries actively helped people in the surrounding communities (mostly rural in the Early Middle Ages, increasingly urban later on) in numerous ways. They worked to educate people and teach useful skills, cared for the sick, housed travelers, and gave food and clothing to the poor. These good works complied with the words of Jesus: "Inasmuch as ye have done it unto one of the least of these my brethren, ye have done it unto me" (Matthew 25:40).

Aid for the Poor

Monasteries helped the poor by charitably distributing food, clothing, and other necessities. The monk who was in charge of these activities was called the almoner. At many monasteries, food and clothing were given out at certain times of the day or week, and people in need knew they could receive help at those times. In giving help to the needy, the monks were expected to be kind and gracious.

Different monasteries carried out works of charity in different ways. For instance, at the Heisterberg Monastery in Germany, a steer was slaughtered each day and the meat was distributed to people in need. Some monasteries allowed people to use their resources, by hunting on monastery grounds or fishing from their lakes and streams. Others handed out stores of grain and surplus crops.

Many monasteries observed the custom of giving special help to the poor on the day before Good Friday, which commemorates the crucifixion of Jesus. Each year on that day, called Maundy Thursday, the monks at Cluny washed the feet of poor people staying in the guesthouse and gave them their shoes. The chamberlain then gave each monk a new pair of shoes, which must last for the whole year. Throughout the year, on other Sundays, the monks also washed the feet of people and gave them money (earned through commercial pursuits such as the sale of crops or livestock or taken in as rent or taxes) as a sign of their own humility and charity.

The Gatekeeper

The portarius (gatekeeper) stood at the outer gate of the monastery. He was usually one of the older and most reliable monks in the monastery. His own cell was located near the gate and near the visitors' guesthouse.

Each morning, the portarius unlocked the doors and locked them again each night. When someone entered or left the monastery, he bowed his head, and, if the guest was a prominent person, he prostrated himself (lay face down on the ground) to show great respect.

Theodoric of Studium (759–826), a Byzantine monk, wrote numerous verses about monastic offices. His "Iambics to the Doorkeeper," found in the St. Pachomius Library, includes this advice about how the portarius should behave, especially in regard to what he should and should not say:

Attend with caution, and with care reply.
Repeat and utter only what is fit.
Be silent on whate'er might evil work.
To those within, without, our brethren here,
And strangers there. Open and shut with care.
Grant to the poor his boon. Or give good words.
Thus when thou goest hence [when you die], thy meed [reward] is sure.

At times, monks carried out more extensive acts of charity. For example, from 1028 to 1033, crop failures in the region surrounding the Cluny monastery led to widespread hunger. Odilo, the abbot at Cluny, melted down and sold some monastery possessions of precious metals to help the poor.

Care for the Sick

Monks were expected to take special care of the sick and the dying, including other monks who became ill. The Benedictine Rule instructed monks to maintain a hospital in each monastery, called an infirmary, mostly for their own use but also to assist others. Benedict wrote, "Receive the patients as you would Christ himself . . . treat each patient as if he were the master of the place."[54] The sick were to be placed in their own room, if possible, and only the most pious and diligent monks were assigned to care for them. Sick monks were entitled to receive baths and eat meat, and were excused from their work and prayer services.

A monk called the infirmerer (or infirmarian) was charged with caring for the sick. The infirmerer, or his assistant, stayed at his post around the clock so that patients could be received at any hour. Mass was recited for the sick in the infirmary, so if the infirmerer was a priest he conducted the service himself; otherwise, he found a priest to do so.

Monks were known to perform surgical procedures and treat sick animals as well as people. They also sometimes cared for people in institutions outside the monastery, including hospitals, hospices (places for the care of the dying), and leprosaria (hospitals for people with leprosy, a disease that caused disfiguring skin lesions). Pope Innocent III (1198–1216) especially encouraged monks to help the sick; to that end, he built the large Hospital of the Holy Spirit in Rome. The Hotel-Dieu in Beaune, France, near Paris, was another well-known hospital where the staff, including monks, nuns, priests, and servants, worked diligently to provide a high standard of care. This hospital received sick, poor, elderly, and maternity patients.

Medical historian Roberto Margotta describes the well-known infirmary at St. Gall Monastery:

Medicines were made up by the monks themselves from plants grown in the herb garden. Help was always readily available for the sick who came to the doors of the monastery. In time, the monks who devoted themselves to medicine emerged from their retreats and started visiting the sick in their own homes.[55]

An infirmerer monk and his assistants tend to an ill patient.

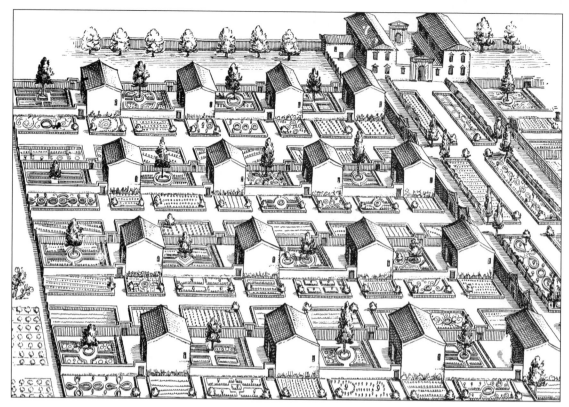

Monks made their own medicines from plants grown in gardens like these.

During the twelfth and thirteenth centuries, the church authorized the building of more and more hospitals and leprosaria. Often, monks and nuns supervised the hospitals and lay brothers and sisters carried out the actual nursing duties.

Improvements in medicine were desperately needed in medieval times, as infectious disease ravaged the European population. Epidemics of measles and smallpox occurred regularly. Diphtheria and typhoid were also common, and leprosy was fairly common. A disease called St. Anthony's fire spread throughout parts of Europe through contaminated rye bread.

Between 1347 and 1351, a form of bubonic plague known as the Black Death swept across Europe and killed nearly a third of the population. There were at least three different types of plague, and all of them were devastating. Infected fleas and rats carried the disease, whose origin was unknown at the time.

Despite their vows of service, monks, along with other members of the clergy, sometimes fled from a plague-stricken area, as did panicked laypersons, instead of staying to care for the victims. The death count rose further when crops were left to wither and die, unharvested, as a result of the epidemic, leading to starvation.

Healing Preparations

Besides giving medical treatments to people, monks also prepared medicines and tonics for

The Black Death

The Black Death, a form of bubonic plague that swept across Europe from 1347 to 1351, has been called the worst disaster in European history. Its devastating lethality caused massive social instability and despair. In an era marked by superstition and belief in magic, people feared humankind was being punished, either by God or by evil spirits they could not comprehend.

Monasteries suffered greatly from this cruel disease, and some lost many members. For instance, at the monastery of St. Albans in England, the abbot, prior, subprior, and forty-six monks all died within a few days'

time. In *Medieval Panorama*, G. G. Coulton quotes Birchington, a monk who chronicled the impact on the people at Canterbury:

"In this pestilence scarce one-third of the population remained alive. Then also, there was so great scarcity and rarity of priests that parish churches remained altogether unserved."

When the plague ended, labor was at a premium, a fact that speeded the end of the feudal system and increased the costs of monasteries that hired outside help.

The Black Death was so devastating that it wiped out entire families, monasteries, and even whole towns.

the sick. Just as they had preserved the history, literature, and languages of the Greeks and Romans, they also retained and disseminated the medical texts of that era.

Cassiodorus, a friend of Benedict and an influential monk, encouraged monks to learn about herbs. Certain parts of the monastery gardens were set aside for growing medicinal herbs and plants. These "infirmary gardens" usually consisted of several raised beds, separated by walkways.

The basic plants for these gardens often came from a list developed by Emperor Charlemagne. In the ninth century, he published a list of beneficial plants that he wanted his gardeners and his subjects to cultivate. During that same century, monks at St. Gall also published a description of the "ideal" Benedictine garden based on ideas from their patron, the Irish monk name Gallus (later Gall) who had lived there during the seventh century. This plan featured a medicinal garden, called the Chirurgical Garden, situated near the infirmary. The monks who worked in these herbal gardens developed special, useful knowledge about growing, harvesting, and using herbs.

One of the best-known medicinal plants of medieval times is Blessed Thistle, a plant used as a remedy and tonic. Also known as Holy Thistle or St. Benedict Thistle, parts of the plant were used to stimulate digestion or to treat stomach upset. The flowers were often brewed into medicinal teas. Tea made with gronsel was used to treat gout, a disease that affects the joints, while a liquid made from yarrow was thought to ease a toothache. Monks also concocted liquid remedies made from plants, alcohol, sugar, and other materials. Some of their formulas came into widespread use, including digestifs, which were used to improve digestion.

Contact with monks who lived in remote places introduced them to new plants and new ideas. Because monks were usually literate and had access to books and writing materials, many of them preserved their knowledge of gardening and recorded information about plants and their cultivation. They also made lists of the items in their gardens during different seasons of the year.

Some pious medieval people believed that prayer would bring about healing as well as, or even more effectively than, medicines or herbs. They asked monks to pray for their recovery or the health of their loved ones. Some pilgrims visited monasteries to pray en route to other holy places.

Safe Havens for Travelers

Monasteries were expected to accommodate travelers, and their locations enabled them to perform this function even in remote regions. In many places, too sparsely populated to support an inn, there was no lodging other than the monastery.

Travel was difficult and hazardous during the Middle Ages. Rich and poor alike had to travel on foot or by horse, donkey, mule, or oxen. Wealthy people could afford carriages but these were also not very comfortable because springs had not yet been developed. All had to contend with bad roads and foul weather, among other problems.

People also had to worry about bandits, thieves, and scoundrels while they were away from home. Englishman William Wey, who wrote guidebooks for travelers in the 1400s, warned that they might encounter dishonest people who "will come and talk familiarly with you and under favor of conversation will rob you."[56] For travelers worried about thieves, rabble-rousers, and drunkards, monasteries provided safer lodgings than many inns and tavern guesthouses. Monastic

Some monasteries provided very comfortable accommodations for travelers and visiting guests. In *Scenes and Characters of the Middle Ages*, Edward L. Cutts, a Victorian clergyman and historian, relates this description of the facilities at Durham, in England:

"Their entertainment was not inferior to that of any place in England, both for the goodness of their diet, the clean and neat furniture of their lodgings, and generally all the things required for travellers; and, with this entertainment, no man was required to depart while he continued honest and of good behavior. This hall was a stately place, not unlike the body of a church. . . . The chambers and lodgings belonging to it were kept very clean and richly furnished."

A knight seeks shelter at a monastery.

guesthouses also were usually both cleaner and less expensive.

To house travelers, monasteries operated guest quarters, along with stables and outbuildings. A monk assigned to serve as a guest-master (often under the direction of the cellarer) was supposed to keep these quarters ready at all times. His duties required him to greet visitors in a cordial and diplomatic way and supply them with necessities during their stay. Because travelers also often needed medical care, some guesthouses had adjacent infirmaries. In some monasteries, it was customary to wash the feet of incoming guests.

Many Kinds of Visitors

Despite many obstacles, medieval Europeans did venture away from home. Monasteries played host to the most exalted monarchs and nobles, as well as knights, burghers, and peasants. Guest quarters were usually divided into four distinct areas: one to receive prominent visitors, a second for poor travelers and pilgrims, a third for merchants who came to conduct business, and a fourth for visiting monks. The abbot usually dined with important guests and sometimes invited senior monks to join these meals, which were prepared in the guesthouse kitchen.

Many travelers were pilgrims on their way to visit a religious shrine, a place that contained sacred relics, or the burial site of a saint or other religious figure. Pilgrimages were regarded as a sign of religious devotion and a way to atone for one's sins, as well as a legitimate reason to visit a new place. Some people also hoped to be healed as a result of a pilgrimage or had vowed to undertake a pilgrimage in thanks for some blessing they had received.

Popular destinations for pilgrims in Europe included the holy shrines at Bath and Canterbury Cathedral in England and the Church of St. James at Santiago de Compostela in Spain. Legend said that St. James the Apostle had preached on this site and the church held his bones. People also set out on long journeys to the Holy Land in Palestine, now Israel. Pilgrims who made this journey in the spring sometimes returned with palm leaves, a souvenir from their pilgrimage.

Although most medieval pilgrims set out for the Holy Land, a number of others went to visit the shrines of saints in Europe. The Rev. Edward L. Cutts describes the preparations:

> Before any man went on pilgrimage, he first went to his church and received the Church's blessing on his pious enterprise, and her prayers for his good success and safe return. [Old records from the British Museum show] at the opening of the service he lies prostrate before the altar while the priest and choir sing over him certain appropriate psalms . . . [and special prayers] for safety in which the pilgrim is mentioned by name. . . . Then he rises, and there follows the benediction . . . and the priest sprinkles the scrip with holy water, and places it on the neck of the pilgrim.[57]

During the journey, continues Cutts,

> the pilgrim was sure of entertainment at every hospital, or monastery, or priory, probably at every parish priest's rectory and every gentleman's hall along on his way; . . . The poor pilgrim repaid his entertainer's hospitality by bringing the news of the countries through which he had passed, and by amusing the household after supper with marvellous saintly legends and traveller's tales. . . . Sometimes the pilgrim would take a bolder flight, and carry with him some fragment of a relic—a joint of bone, or a pinch of dust, or a nail-paring, or a couple of hairs of the saint, or a rag of his clothing; and the people gladly paid the pilgrim for thus bringing to their doors some of the advantages of the holy shrines which he had visited.[58]

The Impact of Monastery Guests

Housing travelers could affect both the economic stability and the social atmosphere at a monastery. Anyone who came seeking lodging or shelter was received, whether or not he could pay. For many monasteries, pilgrims who could afford to pay either with money or goods became a reliable source of income. Some monasteries sold insignia that pilgrims could buy to prove that they had visited their

Monasteries sheltered travelers even if they could not pay, a practice that often strained the finances and resources of the monastery.

site. People also sold objects they claimed were pieces of relics, for example, fragments of a saint's bone or bits of material from a saint's former possessions. Some medieval peddlers made a business of selling fake relics near monastic shrines.

Housing travelers could impose serious financial stress on a poorer monastery, however. A group of wealthy visitors, who were likely to bring along servants, horses, and pets, could be quite costly to feed and house. Some people stayed for long periods of time. Poorer travelers, and sometimes more affluent ones, did not compensate their hosts for all the resources they used. According to Bishop, even rulers

might shortchange their hosts: "King John, after a long stay with an enormous suite at [the English monastery of] Bury St. Edmunds, left as a parting gift only thirteen pence."[59]

Although the guesthouses and infirmaries were kept separate from the areas where the monks ate, slept, and spent most of their time, visitors could still influence the monks' way of life. When monasteries attracted tourists, tradespeople also congregated there to sell them food and other things. Frequent or prolonged contact with people from the world outside changed the atmosphere so that some monasteries were no longer such quiet retreats from society.

Education and the Arts

Although monasteries were not originally conceived as centers for learning or development of the arts, it was natural that they came to fulfill these functions. A number of monks were highly educated men, some from noble and wealthy families that could afford private teachers for their children. As monks, these well-educated and charitable men were naturally inclined to promote learning; in some cases they opened the first schools in a region. For example, in 1055, Benedictine monks at the Millenary Monastery of Pannonhalma founded the first school in Hungary and later wrote the first document in the Hungarian language.

Other monks took advantage of their opportunities to study during their years in the monastery. Literate monks helped their brothers learn Latin so they could read the Holy Scriptures and other works. They also taught the boys who came to the monastery as oblates. Soon, people sought to bring their boys to the monastery for an education even though they did not plan to become monks. (Girls were not permitted a monastery education but could receive an education in a convent.)

The monastery was often the site of the first school in many communities.

Monastery Schools

The Roman scholar and friend of St. Benedict, Cassiodorus, had envisioned these potential roles for monks. Cassiodorus hoped to found centers of higher study in Rome similar to the rabbinical schools of the Jews. According to historian Norman F. Cantor:

> He therefore established a large monastery with the conscious purpose of using it as a center for Christian education and in

his *Introduction to Divine and Human Readings* Cassiodorus carefully outlines a program for the monastic school. The monks were to cultivate the Biblical-patristic tradition [in the ways of the Desert Fathers], but in order to obtain the necessary knowledge of Latin for this Christian scholarship, they were also to preserve and study certain classical texts.[60]

This effort would require that monks produce copies of ancient texts that were not widely available. For this and other purposes, monasteries set up scriptoria and assigned certain monks to work as scribes.

Although secular schools and universities existed in England and such medieval urban centers as Paris and Rome, in many parts of Europe monasteries operated the only schools around. Within two centuries after the Benedictine order was founded, monasteries throughout Europe had established schools, libraries, and scriptoria.

Thus, by the mid-700s monks were educating people of all ages, teaching people to read and write. Most of their students were

The monastery scriptorium was the room where monks worked as scribes copying ancient texts.

Education and the Arts

sons of noblemen and knights, as well as boys who planned to become priests or monks. However, some abbots restricted this educational activity to the oblates.

Monastic studies revolved around religious works, rather than secular literature, and stressed Latin grammar. Some students learned basic mathematics; one former student later recalled his difficulties with this subject: "The despair of doing sums oppressed my mind so that all the previous labor spent on learning seemed nothing. At last, by the help of God's grace and endless study, I grasped . . . what they call fractions."[61]

Schoolmasters could be quite strict. They used a flat wooden paddle called a palmer to smack the hands of unruly pupils. An entry in a book of instruction for monks who taught young boys reads, "If the boys commit any fault in the psalmody or other singing, either by sleeping or in any other way, let them be stripped without delay of frock and cowl and beaten in their shirt only, with pliant and willow rods."[62]

Some men became monks in order to work as teachers; undoubtedly some were less committed to monastic principles than to their scholarly work. At Bury St. Edmunds, Abbot Samson told the monk and historian Jocelyn that "if he could have made bread and cheese by teaching outside, he would never have become a monk."[63]

Scribes

Some monks (and nuns, too) worked as scribes, copying and illustrating manuscripts (from Latin words meaning "written by hand"). Producing beautiful books was regarded as a way to

Most monasteries educated boys and men of all ages but some educated only oblates.

Ornate Designs

Monks who worked in the scriptoria often had time to developed exquisite skills in illustration and embellished their manuscripts with small pictures (called illuminations) placed next to text on the page or added as colorful decorations. The monks who created these works of art were called illuminators. Vivid shades of red, blue, green, and gold were used in the designs. The first letter on each page or chapter of the book was usually an enlarged and decorative capital letter. The borders of the book were embellished with different designs, for example, flowers, vines, leaves, birds, butterflies, ladybugs, or dragonflies.

Different monasteries became known for distinctive designs. For instance, in Celtic manuscripts, groups of small red dots are often used to outline large initials or emphasize a particular line in the text. This technique, called rubrication, was adopted from Egyptian Coptic Christian manuscripts that were brought to Ireland in the fifth century.

glorify God and spread religious teachings to more people. This was considered to be sacred work, for, as St. Bernard told his fellow Cistercians, "Every word that you write is a blow that smites the devil."[64]

Monks also preserved ancient manuscripts written in Greek and Latin that were not religious in nature. They recorded their own history, in the form of diaries and records that are called chronicles. Some surviving chronicles include day-by-day accounts of various events in the region and offer fascinating insight into medieval life.

Scribes worked in a special room called a scriptorium, an important part of the monastery. It was usually located at the top of a tower or existed as a separate building within the closed walls of the compound. Inside, scribes worked quietly at a desk or table, sitting on a stool. Because fire could quickly consume irreplaceable manuscripts, no candles or fires were allowed. Talking in the scriptorium was also forbidden. The monks communicated by using sign language.

Scribes learned to produce letters in an identical hand so that the handwriting of different scribes would be indistinguishable. Often more than one monk worked on the same page of a book. They carefully formed each letter with a pen made from a goose quill or, in the Early Middle Ages, a reed. According to one historian, "The quill pen, which had replaced the reed pen by this time, had to be kept stored long enough for the oil of the goose to dry out; then it was cut and trimmed."[65]

Producing Books

Creating a book in the days before the invention of movable type and the printing press was a painstaking and long process. People who did this work (including not only monks but nuns and scribes whose work was commissioned by the monarchy) required time and patience.

It might take several years for a person to complete one book. The first step was to produce a writing surface. Manuscript pages were vellum, made from the skins of calves, kids, or lambs, or parchment, from the skins

Medieval books took years to produce and were highly valued.

of sheep or goats. Untanned skins were soaked in an alkaline solution of limewater to remove all the hairs, then washed and stretched on frames. The monks then rubbed the skins with pumice stone to create a smooth, thin surface.

The finished sheets were cut to the desired size, and each piece was evenly marked to create margins and straight lines across the page. Space was left for illuminations, the vivid illustrations that decorated a manuscript.

Ink was made by mixing soot with gum and acid. Some ink recipes called for charcoal or burnt bones, as well as acids extracted from dried bark mixed with water or wine. Paint for illuminations was made from the roots and leaves of plants. Special books were adorned with gold leaf. Along with his pen and ink, the scribe held a knife, which was used to sharpen his pen, pare away rough areas on the page, and scrape off any errors he spotted.

Historian Urban Holmes provides a look at the work of the scribe:

The first essentials were a high-back chair with arms, a footstool, and a sort of reading desk on which to place the parchment and the other materials. . . . At times a white cloth was draped over the writing or reading desk. The inkhorn, a genuine cow horn, was placed in a round hole; it had a tight cover so that it could be carried about at one's belt. The vellum parchment was marked off and ruled with a lead point, or simply with a blind point. . . . Anyone copying a book needed to lay a long, narrow strip of parchment into place to mark the column and the line where he stopped, in order to avoid a costly skip of the text.[66]

Many medieval manuscripts were works of art, and surviving examples are treasured

Patron Demon of Calligraphy: Titivillus

Copying manuscripts by hand was not foolproof work, and tired monks occasionally made spelling errors or added or omitted a word. When a monk made a mistake on the page of a manuscript, he could blame it on Titivillus, the "demon" of calligraphy. Supposedly, this demon had started out by collecting the mistakes monks made when speaking during a service, then began collecting mistakes they made as scribes. His goal was to find enough errors each day to fill his sack a thousand times. Titivillus would take these mistakes to the devil, who would bring them out when each monk faced his Day of Judgment after death.

This legend spurred the scribes to pay extra attention and take more care with their work. By the 1400s, errors were so rare that Titivillus was said to have little to put in his sack. In later years, overworked monks who made errors either in writing or in using the printing press blamed these mistakes on Titivillus.

today. They were bound in leather or wood, sometimes with corners or clasps of silver. Velvet, ivory, and beaten gold were also used to cover manuscripts. The books were highly prized and very difficult to replace, so stealing one was a serious crime. Scribes often included a warning to would-be thieves on the first page. One warning from a twelfth-century Bible reads: "If anyone steals this book, let him die the death; let him be fried in the pan; let the falling sickness and fever seize him; let him be broken on the wheel, and hanged. Amen."[67]

Monks also sometimes incorporated personal messages or comments in a manuscript. These might be complaints, such as "thin ink" or "bad vellum." A special brief message at the end of the manuscript, called an "explicit," might simply say, "Thank God, I am finished." Some messages or prayers described the hard work of the scribe and included his name. One note read: "You do not know what it is to write. It hurts your back, it obscures your eyes, it cramps your sides and your stomach."[68] Yet another tired monk-scribe wrote, in Latin, "The job is done, I think. / For Christ's sake, give me a drink."[69]

Arts and Crafts

The production of fine manuscripts was not the only monastic endeavor that used monks' artistic talents. Many whose gifts lay outside the scriptorium became proficient at arts and crafts and various trades, in part to build and furnish their chapels and other buildings, as well as to produce items for sale. Monks encouraged some of the finest craftsmen of their time to beautify religious buildings and produce objects of lasting value.

Some monasteries operated workshops to which young artisans were apprenticed. The monks who taught these useful arts sometimes spent their entire lives perfecting a particular skill, such as a type of metalwork, cabinetry, or lettering. They encouraged those who worked on their projects to obey the laws of the church and to be holy people themselves, for, in the words of the Cistercian St. Stephen of Obazine, "Who builds good churches must himself be good."[70]

Monks were involved in a wide array of trades. According to historian Paul Lacroix, these included

> carving in wood, ivory, bronze, silver, and gold; painting on vellum, glass, wood, and metal; weaving tapestry, embroidering church ornaments and vestments; damask work, and enamelling of shrines, tabernacles, diptychs and triptychs, church furniture, and book-covers; the cutting of precious stones to prepare them for setting; the making of arms and instruments of music, illuminating, copying of manuscripts, &c.[71]

Although some monks, especially reformers like Bernard of Clairvaux, criticized elaborate buildings and adornments in a monastery, others maintained that monks performed a service by creating things of beauty and promoting the arts, including church music and religious poetry. Abbot Suger of the French abbey of St. Denis claimed, "It is only through symbols of beauty that our spirits can rise from things of this world to eternal things."[72]

A monk named Roger of Helmershausen, who wrote under the name Theophilus, added these sentiments:

Many monks felt that promoting beauty through art was just as much a service to God as feeding the poor or tending the sick.

Contributions to Art and Literature

Monastic women contributed to literature and the arts inside the monastery. Like monks, some of them were scribes who copied and illustrated manuscripts. One of the best known of these artists is a Spanish nun, Ende, who helped to paint a manuscript around 786 in Liebana. Diemud of Wessbrun in Bavaria completed at least forty-five books during the tenth century. Hildegard of Bingen spent ten years writing and illustrating her book *The Scivias*, which is regarded as one of the most important religious works ever compiled by a woman.

Other monastic women produced ornate and beautiful embroidery and other needlework, which were used to make the cloth pieces used in churches or vestments worn by the priests who said mass. Nuns also made candlesticks, chalices, and other objects in gold and silver.

Thou hast approached God's house in all faith, and adorned it with such abundant comeliness. In illuminating the vaults and the walls with every diversity of handiwork, and with all the hues of the rainbow, thou hast . . . shown forth to every beholder a vision of God's paradise, bright as springtide with flowers of every hue, and with the fresh green of grass and leaves . . . whereby thou makest men to praise God in His creatures and to preach His wonders in His works.[73]

Critics thought lavish ornamentation contradicted monks' vow of poverty. Yet even the Cistercians, who emphasized humility and poverty, erected some buildings with ornate decorations, such as stained glass windows, fancy tile floors, and elaborate carvings.

Impressive Buildings

The Catholic Church had the resources to build monumental houses of worship and encouraged architectural development in western Europe during medieval times. The church provided the means for sculptors, artists, and artisans to create furnishings, tapestries, metalwork, stained glass, carvings, and other objects of great beauty. Monastery buildings, especially the churches and chapels, show the results of these creative endeavors. Although many of the medieval monasteries exist today, Europe boasts many great public cathedrals that were built in this era, among the most impressive constructions of the Middle Ages.

Early medieval churches had thick pillars, rounded arches, and narrow windows, reflecting some traits from Roman architecture. The style was called Romanesque in continental Europe and Norman in the British Isles. Different regions added their own special touches to the main style, and many churches featured intricately carved doors and sculptures. The Gothic cathedral emerged in the thirteenth century, featuring pointed arches, a vault, and larger windows, often in brilliant stained glass.

In many places, monasteries were the only repositories of fine works of art. At the monastery of Santo Domingo de Silos in Spain, goldsmiths, jewelers, and enamelists all contributed works of art to the buildings. The cloister arcade is richly carved with patterns and biblical animals and birds, as well as scenes from the New Testament. The results of monastic artisans' talents can still be seen in museums, as well as the better-preserved medieval monasteries of Europe.

Operating the Monastery: Material Matters

The earliest monasteries aimed to be self-sufficient; early monastic orders grew their own food and made simple clothing and other things they needed, in keeping with their vow to live "in poverty." Yet, monasteries did receive material goods from men who entered the monastery and from other sources. Adult novices were required to give up their property when they entered the monastery. The Rule of Benedict states, "If he has any possessions, let him give them beforehand to the poor, or, making a solemn donation, let him bestow them on the monastery."[74]

In addition, monasteries acquired money, estates, and other assets from gifts, donations, rents, tithes, school tuition, literary projects, and commercial enterprises. Wealthy families who delivered a son to the monastery as an oblate often donated money and other goods for the monastery's use, such as livestock, fine religious objects, and even the boy's inheritance. People who had received help or prayers from the monks, including travelers, and wealthy patrons provided gifts to monasteries. Princes and nobles sometimes bequeathed property or money to a favored monastery in their wills. Because monasteries could be quite large and served many functions in the community, substantial income might be necessary just to make ends meet.

Sometimes, however, an order accumulated considerable wealth. Although individual monks were not supposed to own property, the monastery itself could own land, money, furnishings, and other assets, which were passed on to each new generation of monks.

To handle an order's financial affairs, abbots appointed monks to serve as treasurer and chief bailiff of the monastery. The sacristan sometimes filled this role. In addition, because the monks had a reputation for honesty, an abbey's sacristan sometimes served as a banker for people living in nearby towns. The subsacristan, his assistant, was in charge of workmen who carried out building chores. Almoners, who were in charge of distributing food and other goods to the poor, were also assigned to look after farmlands under abbey management. They sometimes lived outside the abbey, but their behavior was carefully watched.

Historians have gathered information about the extent of monastic properties by studying medieval documents such as public and monastic records. These sources show that some monasteries acquired great wealth and power. The monks who handled an order's material affairs necessarily interacted with outside society and were often embroiled in political and economic conflicts with, for example, politicians and rulers eager to get their hands on a monastery's assets.

Historian Jean Decarreaux describes the dilemma monks faced in trying to support themselves while adhering to vows of poverty and simplicity:

Labor could not be performed unless there were some place in which it might be performed, and it was therefore nec-

French monks work on their accounts. Some monasteries had extensive assets requiring careful record keeping.

essary for the monastery to possess a certain amount of land which, when well administered, would bear fruit and provide wealth. But in such cases another danger might threaten, for if they were too poor, the monasteries might become debased, but if they were too rich, run the risk of corruption.[75]

Land Grants Bring Prosperity

Monasteries were sometimes the beneficiaries of land grants. The grant of an estate was a gift of great value during medieval times.

Along with the land, the grantee received the other sources of wealth that came with it, such as buildings, livestock, mills and other businesses, forests, bodies of water, and the serfs bound to the property.

Such a gift was granted to the monks of St. Denis in present-day France in 635. Dagobert, king of the Franks, turned over to the abbey twenty-seven estates that included "the villa of Saclas, with its houses, serfs, bondsmen, woods, meadows, pastures, mills, flocks, shepherds, wholly and entirely." The deed indicates the motives of the grantors—"Whatever we have devoutly granted for the relief of the poor, we believe we shall have returned to

Cistercian reformer Bernard of Clairvaux criticized the acquisition of money and power by religious organizations. In *The Penguin Guide to Medieval Europe*, Richard Barber quotes this denunciation Bernard wrote in 1124:

"The church is resplendent in her walls, beggarly in her poor: She clothes her storeys [floors] in gold, and leaves her sons naked. Why lavish bright hues upon that which must needs be trodden underfoot?—And in the cloister what profit is there in those ridiculous monsters of deformed comeliness and comely deformity? . . . In short, so many and so various are the shapes on every hand that we are more tempted to read in the stonework than in books."

In one of his letters, which appears in *A Source Book for Medieval Economic History*, Bernard attacked monasteries that retained serfs and other worldly possessions, saying that these monks were behaving "after the manner of secular persons." He criticized them for owning "towns, villas, servants, and handmaidens, and what is worse, the gains arising from toll duties."

us with profit in the next life"—and states that the grantors make the gift "for the salvation of our soul."[76]

Monasteries with productive farmland were usually able to finance their operations through efficient methods of agriculture and animal husbandry. Rural monasteries often possessed large amounts of land on which they grew several kinds of grains, hay, vegetables and fruits. Many monasteries produced and sold wine, beer, and cider. The location of a monastery often determined its means of economic support. For example, the Cistercian Tintern Abbey in Yorkshire (England) owned sheep farms. Fountains Abbey (Benedictine) and Rievaulx (Cistercian), also located in Yorkshire, became quite prosperous through sheep raising and the sale of wool. Monasteries located in wine-producing regions of France cultivated profitable vineyards.

Hundreds of workers were sometimes required to tend large fields and orchards or care for large flocks of animals. To provide such a large labor force, monasteries brought in lay brothers (conversi) or hired other workers who, in some monasteries, outnumbered the monks.

Taxation and Tithes

Monasteries that owned estates received income from rents the tenants paid them. The peasants who worked on their land provided a source of free labor; others paid the monastery for grazing and fishing rights. The medieval farmer usually had to pay a tithe of 10 percent of all his produce to the abbot who administered the manor on which he lived. This could include foodstuffs like barley, peas, oats, wheat, lentils, pears, apples, and hemp and flax for cloth. According to medieval historian Jean Decarreaux, the annual dues one tenant in Viterbo, Italy, had to pay to the local monastery in 767 included "ten bushels of grain, forty measures of wine, twenty cartloads of hay, and two millstones, failing delivery of which he was without option fined one hundred gold sous, an exorbitant sum which must mean ruin to him."[77] Because the monasteries maintained grain stores, people could also come to them for supplies in times of need.

Abbots of affluent monasteries also received gifts from feudal vassals on certain religious holidays during the year. In some regions, officials also gave monasteries the right to purchase first any supplies that were offered for sale in the towns, such as salt.

While many monasteries collected rents and tithes from the people who lived on their estates, some orders believed this practice went against monastic principles. Cistercian officials declared that they would not accept income from feudal rights or from church property or dues nor use serfs as a source of labor. They set out to support themselves with the income they earned through agriculture and other uses of the land. Lay brothers performed the work. Although the Cistercians often criticized materialism in other monastic orders, some of their houses also became wealthy as a result of industrious members and skillful management.

Different orders continued to disagree about whether it was proper to accept tithes, the services of serfs, or assessments from people living on estates. During the twelfth century, the prominent Cistercian leader Bernard of Clairvaux criticized the monks at Cluny for accepting this type of income. In response, the abbot of Cluny contended that the Rule of Benedict did not make these kinds of exceptions when it stated that novices should give their property to the monastery:

> [The Rule] did not except [exclude] any farm, villa, serfs, servants, or handmaidens, nor anything of this kind. It is clear that

Although members of some monasteries hired peasants to work their land, many others felt the practice conflicted with their vows and that they should work the land themselves.

nothing was excepted. . . . [Since] the writings of [Pope] Gregory contain no exceptions with regard to these things, monks are shown to be able to possess incomes, possessions, villas, and likewise, inhabitants of varied status, that is, free or servile.[78]

The monastery could also sell tithes and taxes to other people, and vice versa. In 1246, the countess of Flanders and Hainault signed an agreement in which she purchased the tithes of property controlled by the monastery of Tronchiennes. In that same document, the countess annulled an annual tax that the monastery had been paying to her, with this decree:

Be it known to all that since we have bought all the tithes of the mills for a certain price from these men of God, beloved in Christ . . . in that same contract between us and them it is agreed that we shall remit part of the price to them and we annul a tax of ten pounds and three denarii which is paid annually to us for the lands named below.[79]

Schools and Books

Monasteries also drew income from students in their schools and from the sale of the manuscripts they produced. In many places, monastery students paid tuition for their instruction as well as fees for their room and board. The parents of wealthy students also sometimes bestowed gifts on the monastery.

The idea of selling the work of monastic scribes occurred as early as the fourth century when St. Jerome (331–420) mentioned that such activity would stimulate learning as well as bring in money. He developed a scriptorium in his monastery, staffed by a group of trained scribes, as did St. Augustine of Hippo and some other influential churchmen. Sometimes, monks contracted to copy a manuscript for a certain price, agreed upon in advance.

Medieval Europeans bought books on religion, history, poetry, science, astronomy, and mathematics. Another popular product was a religious work called a Book of Hours, which laypeople used as a sort of calendar of private devotions. It contained prayers and meditations appropriate for certain hours of the day,

Providing education and books to their communities proved to be a large source of income for many monasteries.

days of the week, months, and seasons. One penny per page was the typical purchase price for this item, but prices differed depending on the size and style of the Book of Hours. Some were small and simple, while others were adorned with coats of arms and elaborate designs and contained personalized text reflecting, for example, the owner's interest in particular saints.

Trading and Bartering

Some monasteries produced items for sale, including textiles, leather goods, candles, liqueurs, cheeses, and medicinal preparations, chiefly from herbs. Sometimes they were able to trade such goods for needed services or property. For example, in 1268, the monks at Beaumont-le-Roger made an arrangement with a noble household. The nobles granted them a small piece of land in exchange for a variety of food—loaves of bread and one gallon of cider or beer each day, one dish containing beans three times a week, six eggs on the other days, and four herring fish during Lent. In addition, the monks were required to give them a bushel of wood every month and thirty sous a year (about twenty-one dollars).

Large monastic orders could also trade within their own organization. One monastery might have a surplus of wheat or timber on its land, while another had plenty of grapes or oats or pigs.

Managing Economic Affairs

Abbots might manage their monastery's assets themselves. An abbot could also name a personal steward to keep the accounts of manors and other holdings, often with little or no interference from outside officials.

This illustration from the Book of Hours shows clergy at a church service.

The administrator or steward of the monastery was called an avowee and held a privileged position in society. The wages for the avowee came from people in the community. In some places, every household in the lands controlled by the monastery was required to pay tithes or dues to the monastery. These might include loaves of bread, grain, produce, wine, beer, small sums of money, livestock, or some combination of these items.

In large monasteries with substantial assets, professional people handled estate management and accounting duties. They took charge of the laborers who worked the land, herded sheep, fished, operated grain mills, or performed other important economic tasks.

Money Problems

Some monasteries did not take in enough money to finance their operations and support their members. Such was the case at

Making Beer and Other Beverages

During the Middle Ages, people seldom drank water, because it made them sick, being heavily polluted with waste products of

every description. Those who did drink water, often put it through a strainer first. Beer, ale, and fermented cider were popular thirst-quenchers.

Beer, the fermented product of barley, sugar, salt, and various types of yeast, was widely available. Some monasteries began brewing beer for sale as well as for their own use. They developed high quality beer that sold well and created new ways of brewing it. In the Brabant monasteries in Belgium, monks found creative ways to use hops in their beer recipes.

Monks also grew and sold herbs that were used in medicinal preparations and brews. One of the most widely used herbal mixtures was gruit, which was used, in turn, to make a drink called metheglin, a form of mead. Mead was an alcoholic drink that had been made since ancient times.

Monks in the Middle Ages made and drank beer; it was healthier than water.

Cluny when Peter the Venerable became abbot in 1124. He later described his monastery's financial woes:

> I found a large church, devout and famous also, but exceedingly poor, burdened with great expenses, and, in proportion, hardly any income at all. There were brethren to the number of three hundred or more, but the house could not support one hundred by its own outlay. There was always a crowd of guests and countless numbers of poor.

According to Abbot Peter, the income Cluny received each year from its estates was

scarcely enough for four months, sometimes not even for three months, and the wine from all sources was never enough for two months, not even for one. The bread was scanty, black, and made of bran. The wine was exceedingly watery, tasteless, indeed, scarcely wine at all.[80]

As a result, the monastery had incurred debts to buy grain and wine, among other things. Abbot Peter set out to improve the monastery's finances. He examined the way the estates were being run and made some cost-saving changes. He also began arranging for different monasteries in the Cluny system to trade various items that were abundant in one region and in short supply in others.

The Abbey of Bury St. Edmunds also found itself in debt during the twelfth century. In the "Chronicle of Jocelin of Brakelond," the following account describes the events that led to that monastery's problems:

> Things outside were badly handled, since each one, serving, under a master simpleminded and now growing old, did as it liked, not as it beseemed him. The homesteads and all the hundreds of the abbot were given out to farm; the woods were cut down, the manor houses went to ruin; all things got into a worse condition from day to day. There was only one solace and remedy for the abbot—to borrow money, so that at least he might keep up the honour of his house.[81]

Whenever he ventured outside the monastery, the abbot of Bury St. Edmunds found himself harassed by the citizens who had lent him money. He felt this obligation personally, saying, "My heart will never be at rest till I shall know the end of my debt."[82]

In many monasteries, monks sometimes borrowed money to fulfill their duties. For example, cellarers might need extra money to buy supplies, and sacristans might borrow in order to repair or replace items in the chapel. Larger numbers of pilgrims and other guests, including chronically ill people who spent their last years in monastery hospitals, came during the Late Middle Ages. They often exhausted the monastery's resources, and, by their very presence, these worldly people influenced life inside the monasteries.

Economic and Political Controversies

Wealth and power put the monasteries in direct competition with feudal lords, merchants,

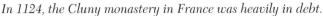
In 1124, the Cluny monastery in France was heavily in debt.

and creditors. At times, they became embroiled in arguments over land boundaries, rights, taxes, tolls, and other economic issues. These worldly affairs were outside the sphere of monastic life as St. Benedict and other leaders had envisioned it.

As they gained control over more property, monasteries encountered resistance from powerful politicians and town officials and residents. These disputes often occurred after monasteries enclosed parcels of land so they could use it for grazing, increase agricultural production, or make other improvements. Residents complained that the monks were curtailing their rights to pass through the area, hunt, fish, or use the land in other ways. In 1254, for example, monks at the Colchester Abbey in England reached an agreement with the local people permitting them to hunt for hare or foxes on parts of the abbey's land as long as they promised to pay for any damage they did to crops.

Many powerful Europeans coveted the assets of wealthy monasteries. During the Late Middle Ages, in Germany, England, and other places, royalty and political leaders took over monasteries. They drove out the monks and used the buildings for their own secular

It was not uncommon for royalty or political leaders to take over a monastery and all its assets.

The Price of Patronage

Founders and benefactors of monasteries often expected special benefits in return. Some founders claimed first rights to the prayers of "their" monastery, or sometimes referred to the leader of the monastery as "my abbot." Some monasteries were required to maintain a special founders' lodging for the convenience of these visitors. A document quoted by Geoffrey Baskerville, in *English Monks and Their Suppression of the Monasteries*, shows that the monks in one house were required to grant to the founder and his "noble ancestors" "our prayers and suffrages and other devout and meritorious acts and good deeds, but all other customs, duties, pleasures and all that doth appertain and belong to the just title and right of a founder."

Dissatisfied founders could try to remove the leaders of a monastery. They could complain to church authorities who might then select another abbot or prior. For example, Baskerville quotes a fifteenth-century English bishop as follows: "The Earl of March complains as patron and founder, that his priory is in a state of collapse. My duty forces me to get the present prior out and have another elected."

purposes and benefited from the lands and other resources. The church hierarchy also took over some monasteries and gave them to ordained clergy.

Some rulers used monasteries for their own purposes. They demanded the right to appoint the abbot of their choice in return for granting certain privileges or gifts to the monastery. Sometimes they installed members of their own family as abbots. They expected these abbots to do their bidding and even exercise their influence with bishops and popes on matters that would benefit the ruler.

Various problems, including economic ones, caused many monasteries to close down during the Late Middle Ages. In some cases, patrons stopped supporting monasteries. Fewer new patrons emerged to build new monasteries or support existing ones. Political leaders also took over some monasteries in their regions when the monasteries experienced financial problems. Many monasteries dissolved or merged with other monasteries during the fourteenth century when the Black Death (plague) swept through Europe, destroying communities and killing millions. With a dramatically smaller labor force, monks could no longer maintain the order's buildings or continue agricultural work and other enterprises as they had done before.

In some cases, politics caused the demise of many monasteries in a country or region. After the Protestant Reformation in Germany in the sixteenth century, German rulers took over church property. After Henry VIII broke with the Roman Catholic Church in 1535, he carried out a dissolution of the monasteries in England. In some cases, the king used violent force to get rid of the monks and their supporters. At that time, there were over six hundred religious houses in the country. King Henry was able to distribute this land and wealth to various friends and noblemen. Some of the monks and nuns who had lived in these places became destitute. As the Renaissance continued, monasticism no longer played such a significant role in people's lives.

A Lasting Influence

The buildings of some medieval monasteries survive to this day, and a number have been restored. Several medieval monasteries have been identified as important cultural and historical sites. These monasteries include Haghpat in Armenia (tenth century), Pannonhalma in Hungary (tenth century), and Fontenay in France, Maulbronn in Germany, Poblet in Spain, and Santa Maria d'Alcobaca in Portugal (all twelfth century).

As the Middle Ages drew to a close, the influence of monasteries declined and their numbers decreased. Yet the monasteries had played a significant role in life of the Middle Ages. At a time when civilization was threatened from many quarters, they preserved culture and helped to stabilize society. Monks copied ancient writings that might have been lost otherwise. They produced manuscripts and historical records that others could then

Maulbronn monastery in Germany is just one of many monasteries which has survived to the present day.

read. Monks also built exemplary farms and gardens, using some ancient techniques and developing effective new methods.

Medieval monks also influenced politics and the growth of civilization, as new towns formed around them. Some educated monks served as tutors and historians for European monarchs. Others were writers and statesmen who influenced the development of law, politics, and the economy. Among the monks who exerted substantial influence on local government were Wibald of Stablo (Germany), Abbot Suger of St. Denis (France), Abbot Henry of Glastonbury (England), and Hugh, the sixth abbot of Cluny. Nine different popes sent Hugh on diplomatic missions to Spain, Hungary, and other parts of Europe. Monks also encouraged politicians to maintain order and to safeguard towns, roads, workplaces, and commerce, all of which enhanced the growth and stability of cities where society could flourish.

These contributions laid the foundation for the Renaissance and the town-centered life that was to come. In the words of medieval historian Norman F. Cantor,

> Monasticism, which had begun as a flight into the desert from the civilized world, became in early medieval Europe not only an integral part of society but a saving force of the greatest significance in the disorganized civilization which followed the Germanic invasions."[83]

Today, though monastic life has changed with the times and new monastic orders have developed, certain orders retain the key elements that characterized the early monastics and even strive to live like the Benedictines, Cistercians, and Carthusians of medieval times. This way of life continues to draw people who wish to experience their spirituality in an intense and unique way.

Notes

Introduction: "Life Orientated Toward God"

1. Quoted in Richard Barber, *The Penguin Guide to Medieval Europe*. New York: Penguin Books, 1984, p. 124.
2. Quoted in Joseph Dahmus, *The Middle Ages: A Popular History*. Garden City, NY: Doubleday, 1968, p. 71.
3. Quoted in Dahmus, *The Middle Ages*, p. 74.
4. Benedicta Ward, ed., *The Sayings of the Desert Fathers*. Kalamazoo, MI: Cistercian, 1975, p. xxvi.

Chapter 1: Schools for the Lord

5. Prologue of the Rule of Saint Benedict, in *The Catholic Encyclopedia*, www.newadvent.org/cathen/02436a.htm.
6. Quoted in G. G. Coulton, *Medieval Panorama*. Cleveland: World, 1961, p. 263.
7. Leonard von Matt and Dom Stephan Hilpisch, *Saint Benedict*, trans. Ernest Graf. London: Burns and Oates, 1961, p. 113.
8. Quoted in von Matt and Hilpish, *Saint Benedict*, p. 115.
9. Quoted in A. W. Haddan and W. Stubbs, eds., *Councils and Ecclesiastical Documents Relating to Great Britain and Ireland II*. Oxford: Oxford University Press, 1983, pp. 120–21.
10. Bede, *Medieval Sourcebook,*
11. Quoted in Mabillon, *Annales Benedictini*, vol. V 1740, in G. G. Coulton, *Life in the Middle Ages*. Cambridge, England: Cambridge University Press, 1967, pp. 106–107.
12. Quoted in Barber, *The Penguin Guide to Medieval Europe*, p. 129.
13. Coulton, *Medieval Panorama*, p. 166.
14. Quoted in Urban Tigner Holmes Jr., "The World of Bernard of Clairvaux," in *The Age of Chivalry*. Washington, DC: National Geographic, 1969, p. 131.
15. Quoted in Dorothy Mills, *The Middle Ages*. New York: G. P. Putnam's Sons, 1935, p. 137.

Chapter 2: "Not an Easy Entrance": Joining the Monastery

16. Quoted in Coulton, *Medieval Panorama*, p. 264.
17. Quoted in Paul Lacroix, *Military and Religious Life in the Middle Ages and the Renaissance*. New York: Frederick Ungar, 1964, p. 315.
18. Quoted in Coulton, *Life in the Middle Ages*, pp. 98–99.
19. Quoted in Mills, *The Middle Ages*, pp. 131–32.
20. Quoted in Mills, *The Middle Ages*, p. 132.
21. Quoted in Lacroix, *Military and Religious Life*, p. 315.
22. Quoted in Mills, *The Middle Ages*, p. 132.
23. The Rule of St. Benedict, quoted in Mills, *The Middle Ages*, p. 133.

Chapter 3: Obedience and Discipline

24. Rule of St. Benedict, Prologue, Section 5, *Catholic Encyclopedia* website.
25. Rule of St. Benedict, *Catholic Encyclopedia* website.
26. Quoted in Morris Bishop, *The Horizon Book of the Middle Ages*. New York: American Heritage, 1968, p. 138.

27. Rule of St. Benedict, Chapter LXIV, *Catholic Encyclopedia* website.

28. Rule of St. Benedict, Prologue, Section 2, *Catholic Encyclopedia* website.

29. Rule of St. Benedict, Chapter LXIV, *Catholic Encyclopedia* website.

30. Bede, *Lives of the Holy Abbots*, in *Medieval Sourcebook*. Available at www.fordham.edu/halsall/source/columba-rule.html.

31. Rule of St. Benedict, Prologue, Section 7, *Catholic Encyclopedia* website.

32. Rule of St. Benedict, Prologue, Section 45, *Catholic Encyclopedia* website.

33. Quoted in Holmes, "The World of Bernard," p. 146.

34. Rule of St. Benedict, Prologue, Section 7, *Catholic Encyclopedia* website.

Chapter 4: Daily Living

35. Quoted in Jean Decarreaux, *Monks and Civilization: From the Barbarian Invasions to the Reign of Charlemagne*. Trans. Charlotte Haldane. Garden City, NY: Doubleday, 1964.

36. Quoted in Polly Schoyer Brooks and Nancy Zinsser Walworth, *The World of Walls: The Middle Ages in Western Europe*. Philadelpha: Lippincott, 1966, p. 29.

37. Quoted in Bishop, *The Horizon Book of the Middle Ages*, p. 144.

38. Quoted in Holmes, "The World of Bernard," pp. 124–25.

39. Rule of St. Benedict, *Catholic Encyclopedia* website.

40. Quoted in Holmes, "The World of Bernard," p. 137.

41. Rule of St. Benedict, Chapter XXXI, *Catholic Encyclopedia* website.

42. Decarreaux, *Monks and Civilization*, p. 358.

43. Quoted in Gertrude Hartman, *Medieval Days and Ways*. New York: Macmillan, 1937, p. 132.

44. Norman F. Cantor, *Medieval History: The Life and Death of a Civilization*. New York: Macmillan, 1969, p. 166.

45. Quoted in Bishop, *The Horizon Book of the Middle Ages*, p. 144.

Chapter 5: "Watchinge Unto God": Spiritual and Contemplative Activities

46. Quoted in Mills, *The Middle Ages*, p. 135.

47. Rule of St. Benedict Chapter XLIII, *Catholic Encyclopedia* website.

48. Quoted in *Lives of the Saints*. New York: John F. Crawley.

49. Quoted in Holmes, "The World of Bernard," p. 142.

50. Bishop, *The Horizon Book of the Middle Ages*, p. 143.

51. Decarreaux, *Monks and Civilization*, p. 228.

52. Quoted in Coulton, *Life in the Middle Ages*, p. 112.

Chapter 6: "Love Thy Neighbor": Good Works

53. Quoted in von Matt and Hilpisch, *Saint Benedict*, p. 115.

54. Quoted in Bishop, *The Horizon Book of the Middle Ages*, p. 133.

55. Roberto Margotta, *The Story of Medicine*. New York: Golden, 1968, p. 36.

56. Quoted in Jay Williams, *Life in the Middle Ages*. New York: Random House, 1966, p. 151.

57. Edward L. Cutts, *Scenes and Characters of the Middle Ages*. London: J. S. Virtue, 1872, p. 244.

58. Cutts, *Scenes and Characters*, p. 248.

59. Bishop, *The Horizon Book of the Middle Ages*, p. 143.

Chapter 7: Education and the Arts

60. Cantor, *Medieval History*, p. 168.
61. Quoted in Williams, *Life in the Middle Ages*, p. 133.
62. Quoted in Williams, *Life in the Middle Ages*, p. 133.
63. Quoted in Coulton, *Medieval Panorama*, p. 580.
64. Quoted in Bishop, *The Horizon Book of the Middle Ages*, p. 144.
65. Quoted in Urban Tigner Holmes Jr., *Daily Living in the Twelfth Century*. Madison: University of Wisconsin Press, 1962, p. 70.
66. Holmes, *Daily Living*, p. 70.
67. Quoted in Hartman, *Medieval Days and Ways*, p. 140.
68. "The Monastic Art of the Scribe," *St. Joseph Messenger*, vol. 6 (1997–98). www.aquinas-multimedia.com/stjoseph/arts.html.
69. Quoted in Bishop, *The Horizon Book of the Middle Ages*, p. 283.
70. Quoted in Coulton, *Medieval Panorama*, p. 561.
71. Lacroix, *Military and Religious Life*, p. 311.
72. Quoted in Williams, *Life in the Middle Ages*, p. 123.
73. Quoted in Coulton, *Medieval Panorama*, p. 559.

Chapter 8: Operating the Monastery: Material Matters

74. Rule of St. Benedict, *Catholic Encyclopedia* website.
75. Decarreaux, *Monks and Civilization*, p. 356.
76. Quoted in Roy C. Cave and Herbert H. Coulson, *A Source Book for Medieval Economic History*. New York: Biblo and Tannen, 1965, pp. 308–309.
77. Decarreaux, *Monks and Civilization*, p. 359.
78. Quoted in Cave and Coulson, *A Source Book*, pp. 300–301.
79. Quoted in Cave and Coulson, *A Source Book*, pp. 389–90.
80. "Regulations and Property of Cluny, 1150," quoted in Cave and Coulson, *A Source Book*, pp. 318–20.
81. Quoted in Joseph Jacobs, *The Jews of Angevin England: Documents and Records*. London: D. Nutt, 1893, pp. 59–60.
82. Quoted in Jacobs, *The Jews of Angevin England*, p. 60.

Epilogue: A Lasting Influence

83. Cantor, *Medieval History*, pp. 170–171.

For Further Reading

Terence Deary, *The Measly Middle Ages*. New York: Scholastic, 1998. Entertaining and colorful book about the Middle Ages for young readers.

Barbara A. Hanawalt, *The Middle Ages, an Illustrated History*. New York: Oxford University Press, 1999. Looks at the major medieval institutions, including monasticism, and the role of the church.

Sarah Howarth, *Medieval People*. Brookfield, CT: Millbrook Press, 1992. Profiles thirteen types of people from the Middle Ages, including a monk.

———, *Medieval Places*. Brookfield, CT: Millbrook Press, 1992. A look at the major institutions where people lived, worked, and worshiped during the Middle Ages.

Andrew Langley and Geoff Dann, *Eyewitness: Medieval Life*. New York: Dorling Kindersley, 2000. Interesting and colorful illustrations show items of everyday life, as well as arts and crafts; not much text and historical context.

Vicki Leon, *Outrageous Women of the Middle Ages*. Chicago: John Wiley and Sons, 1998. Profiles of fourteen influential medieval women, including Hildegard of Bingen.

Sarah McNeill, *The Middle Ages (Spotlights)*. New York: Oxford University Press, 1998. Engaging illustrations enhance this look at the medieval era; includes look at religious life and monasticism.

Works Consulted

Books

Richard Barber, *The Penguin Guide to Medieval Europe*. New York: Penguin Books, 1984. A scholarly account and analysis of major political and economic events during medieval times.

Geoffrey Baskerville, *English Monks and the Suppression of the Monasteries*. New Haven, CT: Yale University Press, 1937. Scholarly look at how both lay and ecclesiastical interference into monastic affairs caused the decline of English monasteries.

Morris Bishop, *The Horizon Book of the Middle Ages*. New York: American Heritage, 1968. A large-format, colorfully illustrated look at various aspects of medieval life; includes chronology of events in various countries.

Polly Schoyer Brooks and Nancy Zinsser Walworth, *The World of Walls: The Middle Ages in Western Europe*. Philadelphia: Lippincott, 1966. A readable, vivid description at the major political structures and events that shaped the Middle Ages; includes profiles of some important medieval people.

Janet E. Burton, *Monastic and Religious Orders in Britain, 1000–1300*. New York: Cambridge University Press, 1994. An examination of British monasteries during the Late Middle Ages; interesting material about the Cistercians, an order that thrived in that country.

Norman F. Cantor, *Medieval History: The Life and Death of a Civilization*. 2nd ed. New York: Macmillan, 1969. Acclaimed history of the Middle Ages, beginning with the fall of the Roman Empire and ending with the Renaissance, by a noted historian; analyzes the impact of monasticism on medieval civilization.

Frederick F. Cartwright, *Disease and History*. New York: Dorset, 1972. A discussion of diseases with major historical impact; material on the outbreaks of bubonic plague, particularly the Black Death, that devastated parts of Europe during the fourteenth century.

Roy C. Cave and Herbert H. Coulson, *A Source Book for Medieval Economic History*. New York: Biblo and Tannen, 1965. Documentary source with materials that detail economic life and enterprise during the Middle Ages; contains deeds, wills, contracts, legal papers, and other records.

St. John Climacus, *The Ladder of Divine Ascent*. Boston: Holy Transfiguration Monastery, 1991. Text and analysis of the "ladder" of steps leading to monastic ideals.

G. G. Coulton, *Life in the Middle Ages*. Cambridge, England: Cambridge University Press, 1967. The author has translated numerous primary sources to show the experiences of medieval people from different walks of life; includes quotations and writings from monks and abbots.

———, Coulton, *Medieval Panorama*. Cleveland: World, 1961. Detailed work by a well-known historian describes medieval life in England up to the Protestant Reformation.

Edward L. Cutts, *Scenes and Characters of the Middle Ages*. London: J. S. Virtue, 1872. Gives colorful descriptions of medieval people, places, and institutions, with emphasis on visual description and quotations from primary sources. Numerous illustrations.

Joseph Dahmus, *The Middle Ages: A Popular History*. Garden City, NY: Doubleday, 1968. Covers the political events that shaped the Middle Ages in Europe and in the Byzantine Empire.

Jean Decarreaux, *Monks and Civilization: From the Barbarian Invasions to the Reign of Charlemagne*. Trans. Charlotte Haldane. Garden City, NY: Doubleday, 1964. Describes the development of monasticism and its influence on social and political life during the Early Middle Ages.

Genevieve D'Haucourt, translated from the French by Veronica Hull, *Life in the Middle Ages*. New York: Walker, 1963. Discusses life in the Middle Ages; interesting information about France and its monasteries.

Marc Drogin, *Medieval Calligraphy: Its History and Technique*. Montclair, NJ: Allanheld and Schram, 1980. Fascinating and detailed look at the work of the medieval scribes and their tools, techniques, and creations.

Bernard Guillemain, *The Early Middle Ages*. Trans. S. Taylor. New York: Hawthorn, 1960. Shows ways in which the Roman Church unified and influenced early medieval society, with special attention to the revival of monastic life in the eleventh century.

A. W. Haddan and W. Stubbs, eds., *Councils and Ecclesiastical Documents Relating to Great Britain and Ireland II*. Oxford: Oxford University Press, 1983. Documents describing activities of the Roman Catholic Church in Great Britain and Ireland from the sixth through mid-sixteenth centuries.

Gertrude Hartman, *Medieval Days and Ways*. New York: Macmillan, 1937. Readable description of social, religious, political, and economic life during the Middle Ages.

Urban Tigner Holmes Jr., *Daily Living in the Twelfth Century*. Madison: University of Wisconsin Press, 1962. Draws heavily from primary sources and medieval literature to describe life in the twelfth century.

———, "The World of Bernard of Clairvaux," in *The Age of Chivalry*. Washington, DC: National Geographic, 1969. A fascinating and beautifully illustrated account of the famous Cistercian monk Bernard of Clairvaux and the house he founded in France.

Joseph Jacobs, *The Jews of Angevin England: Documents and Records*. London: D. Nutt, 1893. Stories of Jewish social, political, and economic life in England from the mid–twelfth century through 1290; includes material from primary sources, such as deeds and monastery records.

Paul Lacroix, *Military and Religious Life in the Middle Ages and the Renaissance*. New York: Frederick Ungar, 1964. Thorough and absorbing look at life in the Middle Ages, including information about people and institutions, illustrated with more than four hundred woodcuts and engravings.

Donald F. Logan, *Runaway Religious in Medieval England, c. 1240–1540*. New York: Cambridge University Press, 1996. Fascinating accounts of monks and other clergy who left the religious life.

Roberto Margotta, *The Story of Medicine*. New York: Golden, 1968. Fascinating look at how the art and science of medicine developed from ancient times into the twentieth century; discusses the contributions of monks and their roles as practitioners of healing arts.

Leonard von Matt and Stephen Hilpisch, *St. Benedict*. Trans. Ernest Graf. Chicago: H. Regnery, 1961. A vivid and detailed account of the life of St. Benedict, founder of the Benedictine order, with many excerpts from the Rule.

Dorothy Mills, *The Middle Ages*. New York: G. P. Putnam's Sons, 1935. A medieval scholar describes different medieval institutions, including the Catholic Church, and describes the organization and rules of a Benedictine monastery.

Marjorie Rowling, *Life in Medieval Times*. New York: Berkely Publishing Group, 1979. Contains absorbing true stories and anecdotes about people and their activities in medieval Europe.

Benedicta Ward, ed., *The Sayings of the Desert Fathers*. Kalamazoo, MI: Cistercian, 1975. Absorbing story of the development of monasticism in Egypt before the Middle Ages.

Jay Williams, *Life in the Middle Ages*. New York: Random House, 1966. A readable look at life in the Middle Ages, medieval towns and villages, and the feudal system.

Internet Sources

"The Monastic Art of the Scribe," *St. Joseph Messenger*, vol. 6 (1997–98). www.aquinas-multimedia.com/stjoseph/arts.html.

Websites

Medieval Sourcebook. Collection of public domain and copy-permitted texts related to medieval and Byzantine history. www.fordham.edu/halsall/source/columba-rule.html.

Rules of St. Benedict, *The Catholic Encyclopedia*. Comprehensive encyclopedia on Catholicism throughout history. Includes entries on famous monks, monastic orders, and related subjects. www.newadvent.org/cathen/02436a.htm.

The St. Pachomius Library. A archive of literature of the early Christian Church in electronic form, includes English translations of the Church Fathers, the acts of the Christian martyrs, the proceedings of the Councils, and lives of the early saints.

Index

abbesses, 34
abbeys, 20
   see also individual names
abbots, role of, 32–33, 83
Adalbert, Saint, 18
Advent, 53–54
agriculture, 19, 44–46
   crop rotation development and, 41
   gardens, 45–46
almoners, 55, 72
animal husbandry, 45
Anselm (abbot of Bec), 27
Anseys de Mes, 41–42
Ansgar, Saint, 18
Anthony, Saint, 10
antiphoner monks, 48
architecture, 22, 71
arts, 22, 69–71
Augustine of Canterbury, Saint, 17, 54
Augustine of Hippo, Saint, 54, 76
avowee monks, 77

Barber, Richard, 74
bartering, 77
Basil, Saint, 11, 53
Baskerville, Geoffrey, 81
bathing, 42–43
Beaumont-le-Roger monastery, 77
Bec, Abbey of, 25–26
Bede the Venerable, 16, 18, 33
beer, 78
behavior, proper. *See* discipline
Benedict, Saint, 13–14, 24
   on abbots, 32
   anniversary of death of, 54
   on cellarer monks, 39

on charity, 55
on humility, 34
on idleness, 43
on rest, 46, 50
on spiritual matters, 48
on testing of novices, 27
see also Rule of Saint Benedict
Benedictines, 23, 24
   see also Benedict, Saint; Rule of Saint Benedict
Benedict of Aniane, 19
Bernard of Clairvaux, Saint, 22, 23, 48, 67, 70
   on income to monasteries, 75
   on materialism, 74
Bertho (abbot of Cluny), 21–22
beverages, 78
Bishop, Morris, 51, 63
Black Death plague, 58, 81
"Black Monks," 23
Blessed Thistle, 60
bloodletting, 46–47
Boniface, Saint, 18
Book of Hours, 76–77
books, 67–69
   copying of, 52
   gardening and, 60
   as source of income, 76–77
   see also scribes
Brabant monasteries, 78
Bruno, Saint, 22
bubonic plague, 58
Bury St. Edmunds Abbey, 66, 79, 83
Byland Abbey, 41

calendar, 18, 53–54, 76–77
calligraphy, 67–68
   demon of, 69

Cambrensis, Giraldus, 42
Cambridge Medieval History VII, 39
candles, 51
Canterbury Cathedral, 17, 51–52
Cantor, Norman F., 46, 64–65, 83
cantors, 25, 48
Carthusians, 22, 35
Cassian, John, 11, 52
Cassiodorus, 52, 60, 64–65
Catholic Church, 8–9
   architecture by, 71
   Rule of Benedict as standard, 18–19
Catholic Encyclopedia, 16, 34, 54
cellarer monks, 38
cenobitism (communal life), 10–11
chamberlain monks, 43
chapter houses, 37
charity, 11, 23
Charlemagne, Emperor, 19, 25, 27–28, 60
Charter of Charity, 23
chastity, vow of, 28, 31
Chirurgical Garden, 60
"Chronicle of Jocelin of Brakelond" (Jacobs), 79
Cistercians, 23
   clothing of, 43
   on feudal rights, 75
   lay brothers, roles of, 39
   sleep practices of, 46
   water power, development of, 41
   see also Bernard of Clairvaux
Citeaux, Abbey of, 23
cleanliness, 42–43

Picture Credits

Cover photo: Scala/Art Resource, NY
© AKG London, 52, 75
© AKG London/British Library, 35, 50, 53, 77
© AKG London/Erich Lessing, 70
© Archivo Iconografico, S.A./Corbis, 38, 61
© Arte & Immagini srl/Corbis, 10
© Gianni Dagli Orti/Corbis, 26, 45, 64
© Darryl Gill; Eye Ubiquitous/Corbis, 41
© Giraudon/Art Resource, NY, 23, 65, 66
© Hamish Park/Corbis, 21

Hulton Getty/Archive Photos, 16, 73
Library of Congress, 59
© Werner H. Müller/Corbis, 82
North Wind Picture Archives, 8, 17, 18, 19, 25, 32, 36, 42, 46, 58, 68, 76
© The Pierpont Morgan Library/Art Resource, NY, 49
© Scala/Art Resource, NY, 29, 40, 44, 47, 57, 63
© Stock Montage, Inc., 12, 28, 31, 78, 79, 80

About the Author

Victoria Sherrow holds B.S. and M.S. degrees from Ohio State University. Among her writing credits are numerous stories and articles, ten books of fiction, and more than fifty books of nonfiction for children and young adults. Her recent books have explored such topics as biomedical ethics, the Great Depression, and the Holocaust. For Lucent Books, she has written *The Titanic, Life During the Gold Rush,* and *The Righteous Gentiles.* Sherrow lives in Connecticut with her husband, Peter Karoczkai, and their three children.